W9-CHQ-732

Essential

Dordogne

by

JOHN BRETT

PASSPORT BOOKS
a division of *NTC Publishing Group*
Lincolnwood, Illinois USA

Published by Passport Books, a division of NTC Publishing Group, 4255
West Touhy Avenue, Lincolnwood (Chicago), Illinois 60646–1975 U.S.A.

The contents of this publication are believed correct at the time of printing.
Nevertheless, the publishers cannot accept responsibility for errors or
omissions, nor for changes in details given. We are always grateful to
readers who let us know of any errors or omissions they come across, and
future printings will be updated accordingly.

Published by Passport Books in conjunction with The Automobile Association
of Great Britain.

Written by John Brett
"Peace and Quiet" section by Paul Sterry

Library of Congress Catalog
Card Number on file
ISBN 0–8442–8891–8

10 9 8 7 6 5 4 3 2 1

PRINTED IN TRENTO, ITALY

Front cover picture: Beynac

The weather chart displayed on **page 109** of this book is calibrated in °C
and millimetres. For conversion to °F and inches simply use the following
formula:

$$25 \cdot 4\text{mm} = 1 \text{ inch} \qquad °F = 1 \cdot 8 \text{ x } °C + 32$$

Contents

This book employs a simple rating system to help choose which places to visit:

✓	'top ten'

◆◆◆ do not miss
◆◆ see if you can
◆ worth seeing if you have time

INTRODUCTION

The serene landscape of Dordogne rarely fails to cast a spell on its visitors

INTRODUCTION

Dordogne, a mild temperate land halfway between the North Pole and the equator, has unforgettable charm. Nowhere else is there such an array of splendid and romantic old castles, nowhere else are there so many ancient and picturesque villages, seeming to have grown from the very ground on which they are built. The valleys of the sparkling rivers are cloaked with Arcadian fields and woods, and above them there are wild uplands, the haunt of hawk and hare. Every little town – there are no big towns – and each quiet village is steeped in history, in the blood of ancient battles. The old churches have seen a thousand years of worship, the markets a thousand years of gossip and barter.

It all adds up to a scenically beautiful, fascinating, liveable and harmonious whole, and, if this were not enough, Dordogne has something else, as impressive and unusual in its way as the Pyramids or the Great Wall of China. Dordogne was the cradle of human civilisation, the first home of *homo sapiens*, and the evidence of man's early life and his first laborious steps towards the light of reason is there to be seen on every side.

As far as leisure activities are concerned, the one thing you cannot do in Dordogne is swim in the sea, but there are many swimming pools, both private and public, as well as sandy beaches on rivers and lakes. There are facilities for boating of all kinds: sailing, rowing, canoeing, and windsurfing. It is ideal country for walking, cycling, birdwatching, fishing in trout streams or in lakes rich with coarse fish. There are many riding and pony-trekking centres. Keen amateur painters and photographers will find subjects everywhere. Sightseeing is inexhaustible, with more than a thousand castles, countless Romanesque and Gothic churches, as well as the many caves and sites of prehistory. If all you want to do is to rest in the shade of an old apple tree in some delightful garden, listening to the hum of the summer insects, and just bestirring yourself for a superb meal with a glass or two of local wine in a nearby restaurant, you could search the world for a better place. Few visitors to Dordogne, if any, have failed to be enchanted by the area.

INTRODUCTION

Defining the Area

The area which is commonly referred to as 'the Dordogne' is simply the most northerly of the five departments (*départements*) which form the administrative region of Aquitaine, covering most of southwest France. More than three-quarters of the department of Dordogne lies north of the river from which it takes its name. South of the river begins the Midi, the great sunny south of France. Dordogne, formed in 1790 when France was divided into 95 departments, was based on the old *comté* and diocese of Périgord, and with a few minor differences has the same boundaries as the old Périgord. In France, Dordogne is an administrative term used in official business and addresses (the department number is 24), and when a Frenchman uses the term La Dordogne, he is almost invariably speaking of the river itself. For most Frenchmen, and particularly the local inhabitants, the region is still Périgord, and this is the term you will hear in reference to the geography, the culture, and the cuisine of this part of France.

It is one of the great attractions of Périgord that its scenery is both impressive and varied. The area consists largely of wild and wooded country, hilly in the north and east, becoming more gently undulating and then flatter in the west and south. It is watered by the Dordogne, flowing from east to west in the southern part of the region, and by three other beautiful rivers and their tributaries: the Dronne in the north, the Isle in the centre, and the Vézère in the east, all flowing roughly from northeast to southwest. All these rivers rise in the mountains of the Massif Central or its foothills, and geographically Périgord is a transitional area between those uplands and the plains which lie around the Gironde estuary into which the Dordogne flows.

These river valleys and the hills between them break Périgord up into many different *pays*, each with its own characteristics. Although it is the third largest department in France, there are no large towns in Dordogne. The capital, or *préfecture*, Périgueux, has a population of about 60,000, including its suburbs. Apart from Bergerac, with 28,000, and Sarlat, with about

10,000, there are no other places which can, except ambitiously, call themselves towns. The other main centres, Nontron, Thiviers, Ribérac, and Lalinde, can barely rake up 15,000 inhabitants between them. Périgord is traditionally a land of peasant farmers, who tend to grow something of everything and to live simply, but quite well, off their own land. If there is a commercial crop it is likely to be grapes, tobacco, strawberries or walnuts. Though tourism has done something to stimulate the local economy, the season is short, and Dordogne still cannot be called prosperous. The people speak the *langue d'oc*, the language of the south. In the past France was divided between the people of the north, who spoke the *langue d'oïl* in which the word for 'yes' was *oïl*, or oui, and on which modern French is based,

Grapes are an important crop in a region which produces some popular wines

[continued on page 10]

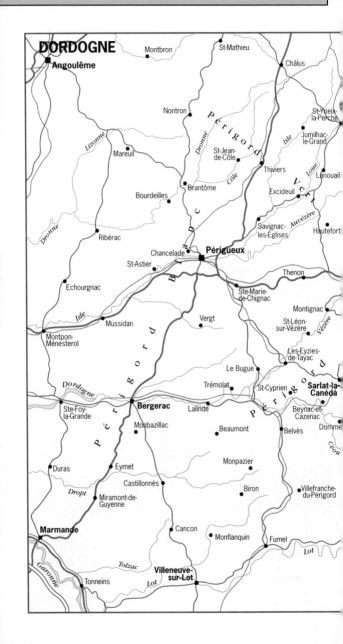

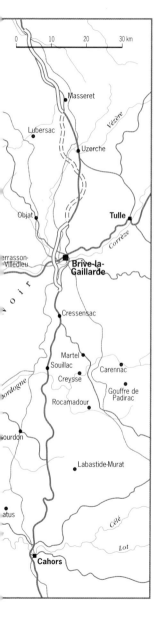

Dordogne

Dordogne is the most
northerly of the five
departments
(*départements*) in the
administrative region of
Aquitaine. Its boundaries
roughly correspond to the
old boundaries of the
comté and diocese of
Périgord. Although
Dordogne is the
administrative term for the
area, most Frenchmen still
refer to Périgord – which
is known and promoted as
three separate regions:
Périgord Vert, Périgord
Blanc and Périgord Noir.
There are maps showing
each of these three regions
on pages 25, 33 and 58–9.

and those of the south, who spoke the *langue d'oc*, in which the word for 'yes' was *oc*. This language, now called *occitan*, is still in common use throughout the countryside of southwest France. Even if your French is very good you will not understand much of the conversation between farmers discussing prices in the famous Saturday market in Sarlat. Most of them, of course, also speak French, but with a very strong accent.

The Different Périgords

It used to be said that there were two Périgords: the White (*Blanc*) and the Black (*Noir*). The White Périgord was named from the frequent chalky outcrops of rock seen in the central part of Périgord, and the Black from the dark foliage of the oak trees covering much of the southeast. But some years ago, the term *Périgord Vert* (Green Périgord), which refers to the northern area, was introduced. In these descriptions it is always the word 'Périgord' which is used; no-one ever refers to White, Black or Green Dordogne. In the past two or three years the wine-producing region around Bergerac has been trying to promote itself as the Purple (*Pourpre*) or even the Purple and Gold (*Or* – because of the white wine) Périgord, but up to the present this term has not caught on, except in tourist publicity.

There are no precisely defined boundaries to these parts of Périgord but, roughly, Périgord Vert (Green Périgord) occupies the north of the department with Nontron as its chief town; Périgord Blanc (White Périgord) is in the centre around Périgueux; Périgord Noir (Black Périgord) is in the southeast with Sarlat as the chief town; and Périgord Pourpre (Purple Périgord) is based on the Bergerac region. People from crowded cities come to Dordogne to relax for a time, or even to settle, because here they find a space of their own, room to move as they will, and time to be at ease and reflect. It is a region of scenic beauty neither remote nor awe-inspiring, but on a human scale which creates a sense of security and soothes the mind. At the same time it is packed with historical interest and a great variety of things to do. This is the magic of Dordogne.

A 20th-century image of Prehistoric Man stands guard over the Museum of Prehistory at Les Eyzies-de-Tayac

BACKGROUND

The story of mankind in Dordogne begins before recorded time, long before men could read or write. It begins with prehistory.
It is not known when man first began to live in the Dordogne area but the earliest flints, worked on both sides to form a cutting edge, are reckoned to be between 300,000 and 400,000 years old. It is certain that men were there 80,000 years ago, living together in small communities of hunters, using caves for warmth and shelter in winter, and probably building rough huts for summer use. By then they were already making wooden spears, bows and arrows, as well as fine flint tools.
Early this century, bones of these men were found in rock shelters at Le Moustier and at La Ferrassie, not far from Les Eyzies-de-Tayac. From these remains scientists deduced that they were about 5 feet (1.5m) tall, had long arms and short legs, and were immensely strong. They had small brains, low foreheads and a prominent lower jaw. The statue outside the Museum of Prehistory at Les Eyzies shows a man of this type. Their intelligence was devoted to hunting and to making the weapons and tools which made survival easier. They are known to scientists as *homo faber* – Man the Maker.

BACKGROUND

This skeleton, discovered during work on a railway in the 1880s, was not a stranded passenger but a 35,000-year-old man

By about 50,000 years ago they had also discovered how to make simple boats and sledges, bone harpoons, and fishing nets. But at some period during the Middle Stone Age, about 35,000 years ago, they were succeeded by men much more like those of today. They were of two different types. The first, identified when three skeletons were found in a rock shelter near Les Eyzies, during the building of a railway embankment in 1868, was named after Cro-Magnon, the local village. Cro-Magnon man was often about 6 feet (1.8m) tall, had a much larger brain capacity, and less brutish features. Experts say that people with typical Cro-Magnon physique can still be seen in Périgord today. The second type was that of a skeleton found at Chancelade, near Périgueux, in 1888. This man also had a much larger brain, but was much shorter and had rather Mongolian features. He is thought to have been a member of a tribe who hunted the many reindeer who lived in Dordogne when the climate was cold. When the animals moved northwards as the climate became warmer, these men followed them and never returned. The men who replaced *homo faber* are known to anthropologists as *homo sapiens* – Man the

Thinker, or Cro-Magnon man. The cave paintings found in many parts of Dordogne were the work of these men, who practised this art for about 20,000 years, between 30,000 and 10,000 years ago.

The Story of the Caves

Périgord Noir has a vast variety of prehistoric sites; the most famous is probably Lascaux. The existence of a cave of some sort was known to local people from the 1920s, when an uprooted tree revealed a small crack in the roof. Access appeared to be both difficult and dangerous, so they called it the *Trou du Diable* – the Devil's Hole – and left it alone. Then, in September 1940, a boy called Ravidat was out walking with his dog, Robot, and three other boys, when the dog disappeared down the hole. Ravidat enlarged the hole with a scout knife and went after the dog. He tumbled down a steep slope, and called to his friends, who followed him. They began to search for an easier way out, and, by the light of a torch, they saw that the walls were covered with many coloured drawings of animals.

They scrambled back up to the outside and, like latterday Huckleberry Finns, boasted to the village and their school-master of their find. The teacher thought they were exaggerating, and got them to take him there. He realised at once that the cave was exceptional, and reported the discovery to the Abbé Breuil, the foremost expert on prehistory of the day. When he had seen it, the Abbé described it as the most important find of all prehistory. But it was wartime, and nothing could be done. When peace came, the French authorities made an artificial entrance to the cave (as that by the roof was impractical), installed electric light, and opened the cave to the public.

People came in large numbers to see the astonishing drawings which demonstrated that, all those thousands of years ago, primitive man had those same qualities that still lead him on: observation, intelligence, resourcefulness, creative ability and the need for a religious belief of some kind. Here, shown in action, were all the animals that he knew and hunted: bison, bulls, bears, mammoth, reindeer and

BACKGROUND

others, some just outlined in black, others coloured in reds, yellows and ochres.

It was not long before some experts challenged the authenticity of the drawings, saying that they could not possibly have lasted 30,000 years. It was soon established that several factors had combined to preserve them: firstly, the roof was covered with a layer of impermeable rock, which kept out all humidity; secondly, the paintings were some way inside the cave system, and protected from changes of climate and temperature above ground; thirdly, in the past, a layer of transparent vitreous calcite had formed on the walls, in effect putting the drawings behind glass.

It was not realised at once, but these stable conditions had been changed by the making of the artificial entrance near the drawings, by the installation of electric light, and by the carbon dioxide and water vapour breathed out by thousands of visitors. By the early 1950s those experts who knew the paintings best began to detect some deterioration in their condition. They were beginning to be obscured by the

Pictures from another age: the vivid images painted on the walls of Lascaux, thousands of years ago

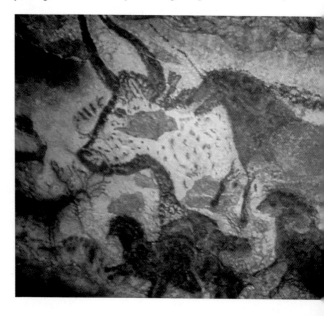

mal vert, or 'green sickness', a form of microscopic plant life whose growth was favoured by the new conditions of more light, warmth, humidity and carbon dioxide. At the same time, increased condensation began to form an opaque calcite deposit on the walls.

In 1963 the original Lascaux cave was closed to the public and has been closed ever since. But to preserve it for science, the cave was fitted with special doors, which create an air-lock to seal it off from the outside atmosphere. At present, only two groups, limited to five specialists each, are allowed to visit the cave. But visitors can see an exact replica of the original Lascaux in a nearby cave (see page 70).

In addition to many hundreds of drawings of animals in Lascaux, there are mysterious signs not yet interpreted, but considered to be indications that the cave was used to practise a kind of sorcery, meant to cast a spell on the animals and make them easier to kill. No tools, weapons or utensils have ever been found in the cave and this, together with the symbols, is strong evidence that it was never lived in, but used only as a kind of temple.

With one exception, there are no pictures of people. But one mysterious drawing shows a bison wounded by a spear, with its entrails hanging out, and seeming about to fall in death. In front of the animal a man, who has just been gored by it, is falling backwards. Unlike the animals, which are drawn with the masterly authority of line of artists who knew every bone and muscle of the beasts they hunted, the man is a matchstick man, like those drawn by children, and has a bird mask instead of a head.

Most of the cave paintings in Dordogne, including those in Lascaux, are believed to belong to the Aurignacian period, roughly 30,000 years ago; but some are as recent as the Magdalenien, about 13,000 years ago. During this long period the technique of the artists developed, so that experts are able to distinguish four different periods of prehistoric art. Because of the limited number of surfaces usable and within reach, drawings were often painted over by later artists, so that the space could be used again, or they superimposed their work on older drawings without painting out. Pieces of wood have been found in some caves, parts of old scaffolds erected to enable the artists to reach suitable surfaces higher up the cave walls. They even lowered themselves on ropes into deeper parts of the caves, and they worked by the light of lamps, usually made from dried moss impregnated with animal fat.

Recorded History

The recorded history of Périgord begins with the Romans, who conquered the whole of Aquitaine, including what is now the department of Dordogne, in 56 BC. At the time the region was already occupied by Celtic tribes, who had a reputation throughout Europe as iron founders. The ore existed near the surface and was easily dug out, and there were large forests to provide the wood for charcoal to smelt the iron.

The Roman presence in Périgord is still shown in the many place names which end in -ac, a corruption of -agus, a common ending of the names of Roman settlements. Examples are Ribérac, Montignac and Monbazillac.

For 300 years the Romans brought peace and prosperity to the area. They linked their towns with the famous Roman roads, always straight, not only because that made the shortest route, but also because they had not yet invented a turning axle. They built aqueducts to bring water to the principal towns. They founded the first spas, and, where there were no natural mineral springs, they filled public baths from rivers or wells and filtered the water to avoid pollution. Even small towns had public baths with a swimming pool, private bathrooms, a gymnasium, restaurants, shops and gardens. The wealthier Romans lived in splendid villas with mosaic floors, fountain courtyards and central heating. They were wine drinkers, and persuaded the beer-loving Celts to plant vineyards, and also taught them new cooking skills.

But the good life could not last for ever. Towards the end of the 3rd century AD Germanic tribes from the north began repeated invasions, and the Roman Empire in the west came to an end in the 4th century. The Visigoths conquered the region in the 5th century, and

The village of Moncaret still provides evidence of life under Roman rule

ruled it for a hundred years. Their chiefs were great admirers of the Romans, and retained their laws and institutions. They left behind nothing of their own but a few place names. Very little is known of the history of Périgord during the centuries which followed. There was an Arab invasion from Spain, but they were heavily defeated by the Frankish leader, Charles Martel, at Poitiers in AD 732, and again in Périgord, near the village which bears his name. It was Charlemagne who finally emerged victorious from the gloom to create an empire which stretched from the Pyrenées to Poland. Périgord was a part of this empire, and Charlemagne appointed one of his lieutenants, Visibode, as count and governor of the province. Charlemagne was a devout Christian and much of his fighting was done to protect or extend Christian influence. He founded a priory at Trémolat on the Dordogne, and, following his example, Visibode founded the abbey of Brantôme in 779 (see page 40).

When Charlemagne died in 814 his empire, built on his military skill and forceful personality, crumbled without him, and once again Périgord plunged into an age of blood, fire and iron, as chief warred against chief.

BACKGROUND

Eleanor of Aquitaine

Eleanor, Duchess of Aquitaine, whose lands included Périgord, is one of the most impressive figures in the region's history. Not only was she the richest woman in the world – she was also glamorous and wilful. She was the daughter of the notorious Duke William X, a villain who would have earned the deep respect of Genghis Khan. Strong, vigorous and ruthless, his only real interests were fighting, food and sex. He was said to eat as much meat at every meal as six ordinary, healthy men, and his sexual appetites matched his gluttony. Eleanor was his favourite daughter and he allowed her to be present at whatever was going on at court. She had inherited his great energy and stamina, and her attitude to men was uncomplicated: the more the merrier. Seeing the opportunity of uniting the huge Duchy of Aquitaine to the kingdom of France, Louis VI was quick to marry her to his son, who soon became Louis VII. But Eleanor and Louis were ill-matched. His idea of a good time was to dress up in a monk's habit and read the lives of the saints. His favourite meal was a bowl of

Rich, powerful and ambitious: Eleanor of Aquitaine, who, with Henry II, ruled England and much of France

porridge. He was physically feeble and not clever enough to meet the demands of government, but he had a certain charm and was chivalrous. In an effort to ensure the succession they had two children – but both were daughters.

No-one could have foreseen what this lack of royal domestic harmony would lead to. In 1151, Geoffrey Plantagenet, Count of Anjou, known as Geoffrey the Handsome, visited the court of Louis and Eleanor, on the face of it to pay homage to his king. He took with him his 19-year-old son, Henry, who, through his mother, Matilda, grand-daughter of William the Conqueror, was heir to the throne of England. Geoffrey's intention was to get his son betrothed to Eleanor's oldest daughter, Marie, who was five at the time. Then, if Louis had no son, Henry would eventually become King of France as well as of England. But Eleanor, 30 years old, bored but still beautiful, took one look at the handsome young man and decided to marry him herself. It was rumoured at the time that she arranged her marriage with Henry while in bed with his father. A divorce from Louis was arranged and on 18 May 1152, Eleanor and Henry were married in Poitiers. Two years later Henry inherited the throne of England. He was already Duke of Normandy and Count of Anjou, so that he and Eleanor ruled not only England, but also the whole of western and central France from the Channel coast to the Pyrenées. Aquitaine, including Périgord, thus became an English possession and remained so for 300 years. Eleanor's favourite son was Richard the Lionheart. She appointed him governor of Aquitaine, a job he took more seriously than his later duties as King of England, which he hardly visited.

Richard the Lionheart captured the fortress which originally stood on the site of Beynac's magnificent castle

Many castles once associated with Richard the Lionheart are still in existence in Dordogne. In the 13th and 14th centuries Périgord still benefited from the prosperity founded in the reign of Henry and Eleanor: the revenues of Aquitaine as a whole were greater than those of the kingdom of England. Not surprisingly, the kings of France cast envious eyes on the region, and eventually went to war with the intention of regaining it.

The Hundred Years War

In July 1324, Charles IV of France sent an army to invade Aquitaine, and most of the Plantagenet territories in the southwest were recaptured. The war continued for 100 years. Like all medieval conflicts, it was fought intermittently. In 1345 an English army under Henry of Lancaster reconquered the lands held by the French since 1324, and a year later the English victory at Crécy (1346) enabled life in Aquitaine to return to normal.

The French continued the struggle, but, in 1356, a small English army led by the Black Prince, son of Edward III of England, completely defeated a much larger French force at the Battle of Poitiers. The French king, Jean, was captured during the fighting, and was taken to England and held to ransom. He obtained his liberty by the terms of the Treaty of Bretigny in 1360, which restored to England all the Plantagenet possessions of two centuries earlier. Hostilities continued off and on for almost another hundred years, depending on the attitudes of the ruling kings at any time. In 1415 Henry V defeated the French army at Agincourt, near Calais, but having proved his worth as a warrior, he lost interest.

The tide began to turn against England when Joan of Arc entered the scene and successfully raised the siege of Orléans in May 1429. The English burned her as a witch, but this drastic action roused the spirit of revenge in the French, and English fortunes went from bad to worse. In July 1453, John Talbot, Earl of Shrewsbury, who had been sent to France with an army of 6,000 men by Henry VI, was killed at the battle of Castillon and his forces were massacred. Apart from this final conflict on the banks of the Dordogne none of the major battles of the Hundred Years War took place in this region, but there is hardly a town or village in Périgord that did not suffer, and does not have traditions linked to 'the days of the English' or buildings which still bear the scars of that time. In Castillon, now called Castillon la Bataille, the tradition is strong, and the final battle is refought every year in an impressively staged spectacle watched by tourists and local residents in their thousands.

The Wars of Religion

In the 16th and 17th centuries Périgord suffered again, in the bloody struggles of the Wars of Religion, Catholic against Protestant, waged all over France. The struggle was intense in the southwest, at that time part of the kingdom of Navarre. Many towns in the southwest, including Bergerac, were strongly Protestant and were repeatedly sacked, captured, and recaptured. When the last of Catherine de Medici's sickly sons, Henri III of France, was assassinated, the Valois line came to an end. The heir to the throne was Henri III of Navarre, direct descendant of Louis IX of France. He had been brought up as a Protestant by his mother, Jeanne d'Albret, and his right to the throne was bitterly contested by the Catholics, who would have preferred a republic to a Protestant king. He disposed of their objections by becoming a Catholic, and became Henri IV of France. The Edict of Nantes, which Henri signed in 1598, gave the Protestants considerable freedom of worship and brought the bitter struggle to an end, at least for a time. But in 1610 Henri IV was assassinated. His son Louis, the child of his second wife, Marie de Medici, was only nine years old, and his mother became Regent during his minority. Religious conflict soon broke out again. In 1620 several Protestant strongholds in Périgord, among them Bergerac, were retaken by the Catholics.

Protestants and Catholics fought bitterly during the Wars of Religion for possession of Périgord towns such as Bergerac

Quieter Times

In 1637 a man was broken on the wheel in the town square of Monpazier, a small *bastide* (walled village) in the south of Dordogne. His name was Buffarot, and he was a weaver who had led an 8,000-strong force of peasants through the countryside attacking castles. This peasant's revolt was the last real violence in Périgord for a long time.

Though the French Revolution, in the last decade of the 18th century, caused serious disturbances in the nearest large town, Bordeaux, in Périgord, with its small towns and villages and thinly scattered population, it caused little impact. The few anti-landlord demonstrations by small groups were more token gestures than real revolution.

When Napoleon made France an Empire that, too, was apathetically received. The restoration of the Monarchy in 1815 was of little concern, except to those peasants whose harvest had been bad. They demonstrated against it.

Life in Périgord had for centuries been based on farming, and during the 19th century this continued to be the case. The Bordeaux wine trade, which included the export of wines from the Dordogne region, expanded steadily, and this helped to improve the economy of Périgord. In 1850 the railway line from Limoges to Bordeaux was routed through Périgueux, which became an important centre for goods traffic. But the main lines from Paris to Bordeaux and from Paris to Toulouse passed well to the west and the east of Périgueux, and left Dordogne to its peaceful country life with very little industry. The pattern has not changed a lot during the past hundred years. Even the rapid expansion of road transport and private motoring since World War I had little effect on the region. It was not until 1983 that it was felt necessary to improve the N21, the main north–south route through Dordogne connecting Limoges to Agen, via Périgueux and Bergerac. This improvement is still going on.

Today Dordogne remains a strongly agricultural department with not much industry. There is expansion in some areas of the economy, but only tourism and its allied services can be said to flourish.

PÉRIGORD VERT (GREEN PÉRIGORD)

Whether you drive into Dordogne from the north by the N21 from Limoges, which is the route most likely to be used if coming from Paris or the eastern Channel ports, or by the D675, which runs slightly further west, you will arrive in the department in the area known as the Périgord Vert. The chief centres in this region are Thiviers, Nontron, and the village of Excideuil.

WHAT TO SEE

NONTRON

This is generally regarded as the capital of the Périgord Vert. It is one of the most spectacularly sited towns in Dordogne, occupying a narrow promontory between the gorges of the fast-flowing Bandiat and one of its tributaries. It is a typical country town, like Thiviers (see below), but orientated towards locally inspired industries rather than agriculture. Waterpower from the River Bandiat has been used in sawmills, and flour milling, and in a knife-making industry. Nontron also has slipper, clog and furniture-making factories. Nontron has two points of interest for tourists. The **Grand Hôtel**, 3 place Alfred Agard (tel: 53 56 11 22) has a restaurant which offers good value regional menus. And, secondly, the town has a museum of dolls and toys in the **Château de Nontron** (open: morning and afternoon 1 February to 15 December: daily, 1 July to

Nontron: a pretty country town, capital of the Périgord Vert

7 September; *closed*: Tuesday at other times). Nontron can be reached from the Grottes de Villars or Puyguilhem (see page 27) by a scenic woodland road, (D707), via St-Pardoux-la-Rivière

THIVIERS

at the crossroads of the N21 Limoges–Périgueux and the D707 Nontron–Excideuil
Thiviers is a market town well known for *foie gras* – there is a small museum to its production besides the Tourist Information Office – walnuts, and truffles, situated on a promontory at the limits of Périgord Vert and Périgord Blanc. To the north, with an average elevation of about 1,000 feet (300m), is the plateau of Périgord Vert, cut by the narrow and wooded valleys of numerous streams. To the

southwest, the ground slopes gently down to the region of Périgord Blanc, with more open valleys.

Thiviers is a genuine country town, living essentially as it has done for hundreds of years.

Accommodation

The town itself has only one small family hotel, the **France et Russie**, 24800 Thiviers (tel: 53 55 17 80), simple, pleasant and very reasonably priced, but without a restaurant. The **Hôtel des Voyageurs**, 24800 Thiviers (tel: 53 55 09 66) is a slightly larger commercial hotel with basic standards of comfort.

If you prefer something more upmarket, the **Château de Mavaleix**, a little north of Thiviers and just off the N21, has spacious rooms at moderate

Thiviers' life and charm have been unchanged for centuries

prices, and a fairly expensive restaurant (tel: 53 52 82 01).

Restaurants

Thiviers has a good little restaurant for a lunch stop, the **Auberge de St-Roche** (tel: 53 55 00 11), which offers good value regional cooking.

Excursions from Thiviers

◆◆◆
CHÂTEAU DE HAUTEFORT ✓

off D704, 10½ miles (17km) south of Lanouailles

One of the most splendid châteaux in Périgord, Hautefort is in a natural site for a fortification, overlooking the countryside for many miles in every direction. Even in the 12th century there was a fortress here, home of one of the great troubadours, Bertran de Born.

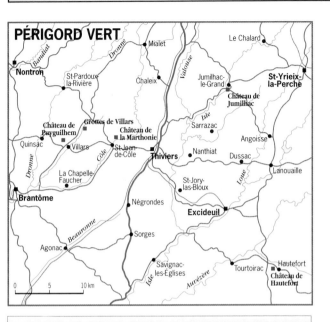

PÉRIGORD VERT

Troubadours

Twelfth-century Périgord saw the creation of a new form of lyrical poetry, the work of the troubadours, travelling artists who entertained the courts of the area's feudal lords. The name of the troubadours – whose art included music and singing as well as poetry – derives from the Occitan word *trobar* – 'find' – as the artists 'found' (or invented) the new poems.

Troubadours are most famous for their love poetry – usually a highly romantic ballad to the beauty and gentleness of the lady of the castle – which exactly fitted the mood of early medieval France, where images of chivalry and courtliness overlaid the often brutal conflicts between great lords.

However, the troubadours not only sang of love, but of the heroes of war and the inadequacies of certain leaders. One of the greatest of the troubadours was Bertran de Born whose home was the Château de Hautefort. This unusual man, who was both a poet and soldier, was an implacable enemy of the English rulers of Aquitaine, particularly Richard the Lionheart. Bertan de Born, who composed charming songs to please the ladies of the court, was also a master of what was called the *sirvente*, a kind of blistering medieval calypso which ridiculed the weaknesses and mistakes of those in power, and was as feared by them as any weapon.

PÉRIGORD VERT

Survivor of fire and neglect: the restored Château de Hautefort

Bertran's castle was destroyed on the orders of his brother who supported Richard. Heartbroken, Bertran became a monk. The castle was rebuilt in the 17th century by Jean François de Hautefort. It is a magnificent building, not only large and imposing, but also elegant and well proportioned, and worthy of comparison with the better châteaux of the Loire.

A fine park of 74 acres (30 hectares) and attractive gardens surround the castle. In 1929, when the castle was bought by the de Bastard family, it was in a dilapidated condition, having been neglected for many years. They spent a lot of money and time in restoring it, only to have it damaged by fire in 1968. They stubbornly set to work again, this time with State aid.

Hautefort contains some excellent 17th- and 18th-century furniture, fine tapestries, and the altar which was used for the coronation of Charles X at Reims.

Open: morning and afternoon, June to mid-November.

◆◆
CHÂTEAU DE JUMILHAC LE GRAND
about 12 miles (19km) northeast of Thiviers by the N21 and D78

The Château de Jumilhac le Grand, with its many towers and pepper-pot turrets, dominates the town of Jumilhac from a rocky outcrop above the River Isle. The oldest part of the building dates from the 13th century; two wings were added in the 17th. The Grand Hall has a splendid chimney-piece with sculptures representing the four seasons, and in one of the round towers there is a stone staircase

with Louis XV balusters.
The castle, which looks as if it
might have been designed by
Walt Disney, has its own legend.
In one of the towers a spiral
staircase leads to a room known
as the Spinner's Room, after a
former chatelaine of the castle,
Louise de Hautefort, who was
imprisoned here by her
husband in punishment for her
infidelity. She passed her time
spinning wool and weaving
tapestries to decorate the room
with wool brought by a noble
lover disguised as a shepherd.
How the matter was resolved is
not certain, some say the lover
was caught and killed by the
husband, others that the
thwarted lover became a monk.
To reach the castle, follow the
N21 for 2½ miles (4km) north of
Thiviers and then take a right
fork, the D78. For most of the
9 miles (15km) to Jumilhac this
picturesque road follows the
winding course of the River Isle.
Open: morning and afternoon,
July to mid-September, and on
Saturdays, Sundays and public
holidays throughout the year.
Monday and Wednesday
afternoons from October to May.

◆◆
CHÂTEAU DE PUYGUILHEM
*off the D98 west from St-Jean-de-
Côle*
This early Renaissance castle
was built by Mondot de la
Marthonie, president of the
Bordeaux parliament, during the
16th century. It is remarkable for
its overall harmony and the
refinement of its sculpture.
When it was bought by the State
in 1939 it had been long
neglected and was almost a

ruin. It was restored by the
Department of Historical
Monuments between 1945 and
1958. What you see today owes
much to the skill with which this
work was done. The interior of
the château is furnished with
antiques donated by various
national museums. It retains its
original monumental chimney-
pieces, the finest of which, with
sculpture showing six of the
Labours of Hercules, is in the
Great Hall on the first floor.
Open: morning and afternoon,
1 July to 7 September.
Closed: Tuesday during the rest
of the year, and from 16
December to 31 March.

◆
EXCIDEUIL
southeast of Thiviers on the D76
A small but busy little place,
Excideuil has a good market on
Thursdays. It has the remains of
a 12th-century fortress, to which
was added a Renaissance
mansion by a member of the de
Cars family (see **Château les
Milandes**, page 64) in the 16th
century. The property passed to
the Talleyrand family in 1613.
The castle is not accessible to
the public, but a pleasant walk
around the ruins is possible.
Excideuil was the home of
Marshal Bugeaud, the man who
conquered Algeria. He is
commemorated by a fountain in
the town centre.

◆
GROTTES DE VILLARS
*2 miles (3km) from
Puyguilhem, via the village of
Villars and the D82*
The Grottes de Villars, or
Grottes de Cluseau, are

interesting caves which contain brilliant yellow ochre and white stalactites and other strange rock formations. On some walls there are prehistoric paintings from the Aurignacian period, about 20,000 years ago, their authenticity proved by the layer of calcite which has preserved them.

Open: all day, July and August; afternoons only, April to June, September and October.

◆◆
ST-JEAN-DE-CÔLE
4 miles (7km) west of Thiviers by the D707
St-Jean-de-Côle is a village which will please photographers and artists. It is picturesque and charming without being twee, and has a number of interesting buildings, including a Romanesque church, a Renaissance priory, a part-Renaissance château, and an old covered market, all grouped around the main village square. The church, formerly part of an Augustinian priory, is an attractive building dating from the 11th century. The nave was roofed for many years with the second largest dome in Périgord, but after it had collapsed twice it was replaced in the 19th century by a pitched wooden roof.

All that remains of a 12th-century castle is the tower and foundations, but the **Château de**

la **Marthonie**, rebuilt in the 15th and 16th centuries, is open to the public morning and afternoon during July and August. Its most interesting feature is a fine staircase added in the 17th century. The adjoining priory, which can be visited at the same time as the château, has substantial remains of a 16th-century cloister. In the streets off the village square there are some medieval houses dating from the 12th to the 14th centuries. Altogether, St-Jean-de-Côle, with its fascinating varied roofscape of reddish brown tiles, its ancient buildings, and the little

A Périgord village at its best:
St-Jean-de-Côle's quiet beauty

River Côle idling through the village and crossed by an old hump-backed bridge with cutwaters, is an enchanting place.

◆
TOURTOIRAC
6 miles (10km) west of Hautefort
on the other side of the D704
The village of Tourtoirac is set on the banks of one of the Dordogne's prettiest rivers, the Auvézère. Tourtoirac is the last resting place of one of the 19th century's many strange adventurers, Antoine Orélie de Tounens. By profession he was a lawyer in Périgueux but, like many office-bound men before and since, he dreamed of greater things. In 1858 he borrowed money and set sail for the far south of the American continent, intending to form his own colony there and attach it to France. He did succeed in persuading some Patagonian tribes to accept him as their chief, and he named himself King of Auracania. The Chilean authorities, who unsportingly regarded the territory as already theirs, were not much impressed and sent him packing back to France. Nine years later he tried the same thing again and, if the Patagonians were glad to see their king back, the Chileans were not. He was again returned to France. But Orélie-Antoine I had a touch of royal single-mindedness about him and he tried twice more but the end result was the same: failure. He returned to France and died in Tourtoirac in 1878.
The village once had a Benedictine Abbey, of which

The ivy-clad remains of a Benedictine Abbey, at Tourtoirac

some of the 14th-century fortifications, some of the abbey living quarters, and the church, part-Romanesque and part-Gothic but much restored, still exist.

Accommodation

The **Hôtel des Voyageurs**, route de Périgueux (tel: 53 51 12 29), does a good country lunch at a moderate price. There are many hotels of this name in France, and they often offer good value. They had to, because they were set up for commercial travellers, or *voyageurs*. These days they are more usually called *représentants*, but the sign VRP (*Voyageurs, Représentants, Placants*) outside a country hotel is still a recommendation of value for money. These clients get a reduction on the charges, which are reasonable to start with.

PÉRIGORD BLANC (WHITE PÉRIGORD)

Périgord Blanc, or White Périgord, occupies the centre and southwestern parts of the department, around Périgueux, Bergerac, and Ribérac. Its name is said to be derived from the chalky outcrops of limestone visible in the less forested areas, most noticeably around St-Astier (there are no physical or official boundaries to these different sections of Périgord).

WHAT TO SEE

BERGERAC

57 miles (92km) east of Bordeaux, on D936 and 25 miles (40km) south of Périgueux by the N21

Bergerac is an important crossroads and commercial centre, and the largest town on the banks of the Dordogne. Its development began with the construction of a castle, since disappeared, in the 11th century, and the building of a bridge across the river about a hundred years later. This was the only permanent crossing of the Dordogne for a long time, and made Bergerac a natural link between northern Périgord and the Bordeaux region. For hundreds of years there was no bridge across the wide Gironde, the combined estuary of the Garonne and the Dordogne, and Bordeaux was on the south side. The local people were soon exporting their wines to the Bordeaux merchants who sent them on to England, but this prosperous trade was interrupted by the Hundred Years War, in which Bordeaux was deeply involved. From 1345 it was English for 30 years, from 1377 French for 30 years, then English again, and then French again. When the war was over, Bergerac enjoyed a period of steady growth, interrupted by several outbreaks of the plague in the early 16th century.

Bergerac was a staunchly Protestant town when the religious wars broke out, and, despite constant persecution, the inhabitants refused to abandon the new faith. Many of them chose instead to move to more tolerant parts of Europe, or to America. This emigration increased after the Edict of Nantes, which had allowed Protestants freedom of worship, was revoked in 1685. The population of Bergerac dropped sharply and its economy suffered.

As the religious conflict died down, Bergerac recovered, and, by the time of the French Revolution, it had become the most important place in Périgord, with a population of 8,000 against the 7,000 of Périgueux – figures which, in themselves, indicate the rural nature of Dordogne in those days. But during the 19th century new main roads were built, linking Bordeaux to Paris via Limoges, well away from Bergerac. The coming of the railway favoured Périgueux, and reduced the importance of Bergerac as a north-to-south crossing place. Gradually, Périgueux became much the more important town, while

PÉRIGORD BLANC

Bergerac stagnated through the major part of the century. It was the establishment of a government explosives factory and the development of a tobacco industry that gave the town a new impetus. In recent times its old wine industry has also considerably expanded. Bergerac today is an active business centre, offering services of all kinds to the southern part of the department. It is a shopping centre for the agricultural area that surrounds it, and has large and colourful markets where as many as 500 farmers bring their produce. Today, not much evidence remains of Bergerac's colourful past. It is pleasantly situated on a south-facing slope above the north bank of the Dordogne, but, as a town with neither castle nor cathedral, it lacks a focal point of interest. In recent years an active restoration programme has succeeded in making the surviving parts of the **old town**, near the river, well worth visiting. This area, now mostly pedestrianised, contains a number of old timbered buildings, including the **Vieille Auberge** in the rue des Fontaines, originally 14th-century. In the 17th-century Maison Peyrarède there is a comprehensive museum of tobacco: the **Musée du Tabac** examining the social and medicinal use of tobacco, with examples of pipes, snuffboxes and works of art with a smoking theme. There is a small museum recording the town's history in the adjacent house. Both are open daily, except Mondays and Sunday mornings.

In the nearby place de la Myrpe there is a museum which is perhaps more likely to interest

Renovation has brought new interest to Bergerac, a town with a lively past

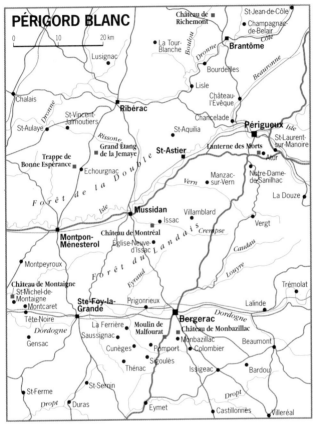

PÉRIGORD BLANC

the average tourist. It has an evocative collection on the local wine industry, together with exhibitions on cooperage (barrel-making) and on the *gabardes*, the flat-bottomed boats used to move the barrels downriver. The museum is open morning and afternoon, Tuesday to Friday, and on Saturday mornings.

There is a statue in the **Place de la Myrpe**, and a remarkably successful one it is. It cannot have been easy to preserve the boastful swagger of the typical Gascon in stone, but in the dramatic sweep of the cloak, the challenging tilt of the head, and the long, defiant nose, the sculptor has achieved it admirably. It represents Cyrano de Bergerac, the touchy, swashbuckling swordsman hero of Edmond Rostand's perennial play.

PÉRIGORD BLANC

Cyrano de Bergerac

The man most associated with the town of Bergerac did not come from the town and never went there. He was, however, a real person. His original name was Savinien Cyrano, born in Paris of Italian family in the 17th century. He became a professional soldier and was posted to a regiment of Guards commanded by Monsieur Carbon de Casteljaloux, a Gascon whose men were almost all impoverished sprigs of the Gascon nobility. In order to fit in better with them, Cyrano added the 'de Bergerac' to his name. Some say that he was thinking of a small family property called Bergerac in the country near Paris. In addition to being a soldier, he was a poet and playwright of considerable ability. He was also a superb swordsman and fought countless duels. He died in 1655. It was 250 years later that he was born again in Edmond Rostand's play as a swaggering Gascon ready to fight on any pretext. The play was one of the most immediate and universal successes in the history of the French theatre. With considerable poetic charm, Rostand tells the story of a brave and noble-hearted man whose life and loves are made impossible by his enormously long nose. Insults, real and imagined, oblige him to fight countless duels in defence of his honour. He is amorous, but women laugh at him, and though he loves the pretty Roxane, the closest he can get to her is to write love letters for his friend, who also fancies her. Rostand graced this sad and sentimental tale with a style and poetic flair that made it genuinely moving and widely popular. It made his fortune. The men of Bergerac are quick to see an advantage, and when the facts of Cyrano's origin were discovered and pointed out to them, they brushed them aside with a shrug. After all, they say, he is Cyrano de Bergerac, *n'est pas?* So Bergerac still has its hotel, restaurants, bars, cinema, etc Cyrano, and the statue, and is not likely to part with them.

Cyrano, Bergerac's adopted hero

Also in the old quarter is Bergerac's **Maison du Vin**, installed in the former Monastery of the Récollets. This was originally the base of the Catholic fathers who, backed by royal troops, were sent by Louis XIII with the task of re-converting Protestants to the Catholic faith. The word *récollets* is derived from the verb *récoller* which means 'to stick back together', and this was what these priests were meant to do to the divided Christian faith in Bergerac. They failed.

The Maison du Vin has an inner courtyard, the former cloister, and there is a fine vaulted cellar where meetings of the Winemaker's Guild are held. On the first floor there is an ornate Great Hall, with views of the Monbazillac vineyard. The Maison du Vin is open to the public daily in July and August.

Accommodation

Hôtel La Flambée, Pombonne, route de Périgueux (tel: 53 57 52 33) is a Logis de France. An attractive hotel with an excellent garden restaurant is **Hôtel Le Bordeaux**, 38 place Gambetta (tel: 53 57 12 83). Another Logis de France, in the centre of town, but with a garden and swimming pool.

Near Bergerac
Manoir Grand Vignoble, St-Julien de Crempse 24140 (tel: 53 24 23 18). An up-market hotel and sports complex on a country estate, 7 miles (12km) north of Bergerac by the N21 and D107. Good restaurant (closed Christmas Eve to 1 February). Hotel open all year.

Medieval houses grace the revived old town in Bergerac

Restaurants
Bergerac has some sound restaurants. **Le Cyrano**, 2 boulevard Montaigne (tel: 53 57 02 76), a small restaurant with high standards, but noisy situation.

Brasserie Royal Périgord, boulevard de la Résistance (tel: 53 57 24 90) is a typical small town brasserie with meals at moderate prices.

It is worth driving a few miles out of Bergerac to either La **Grappe d'Or**, on the Marmande road, intersection of D17 from Sigoules (good, professional, but not expensive); or **La Tour des Vents** (tel: 53 58 30 10), near Moulin de Malfourat on the D933 south of Bergerac (good food and magnificent views from the garden towards Bergerac).

PÉRIGORD BLANC

Visits to Vineyards

The good red wines of Pécharmant are produced on the hillsides northeast of Bergerac, but most of the wines which have contributed so much to the economy of Périgord over the centuries come from extensive vineyards south of the river.

The village which gives its name to Monbazillac, the most important wine of this region, is only a few miles south of Bergerac. It was first exported in the 13th century, and has been famous for so long that, when one of the Popes of the Middle Ages once asked where Bergerac was, he was told 'very close to Monbazillac'.

The **Château de Monbazillac** is now the property of the local wine co-operative. It is an attractive castle, built in 1558, which, fortunately, has survived without damage through all the troubles in the area. It is a fine example of the transitional period between the solid, defensive castle and the more refined *château de plaisance*, like those on the River Loire. It is rare, in that it has never been altered, and what you see today is what François Aydié had built

Périgord Blanc is wine country; the vineyards of the Château de Monbazillac produce a fine example

in 1558. It is well worth a visit, with some fine rooms, a small wine museum plus a collection of folk art and *périgourdin* furniture. From the château's northern terrace, there is an excellent view of the local vineyards and, beyond them, of Bergerac. From 1 June, for the summer season, there is a good restaurant for lunches and dinners (tel: 53 57 06 38). Open for visits and wine-tastings on weekdays all year round.

Not far from Monbazillac, there are two vineyards with English associations: one from long long ago, one more recent. According to some, the **Château de Planques** may be the origin for the use of the word 'plonk' for ordinary table wine. These vineyards, beside what is now the N21 south of Bergerac, have produced wine for a very long time, and were always on this

A gift of love, and a house of wine: the Château de la Jaubertie

main route south from Bergerac. It is likely that their wine was drunk by English soldiers during the Hundred Years War. There is no historic building there now, but the name is related to the old French word *planque*, passed into English as plank, and refers to the simple wooden footbridge across the tiny stream that runs through the vineyard, and which has always been there. Today, the château produces acceptable reds and a rather good value dry white made from the Sauvignon grape. The connection may be tenuous, or even imaginary, but if you want to amuse your friends with a genuine bottle of 'plonk' and a good story, this is the place to come.

Nearby, at Le Colombier, there is a positive English connection. The **Château de la Jaubertie** was taken over some years ago by Nicholas Ryman, a member of the well-known stationery and office supplies family who sold up and added to the long tradition of Britons who have come to southwest France to make wine or brandy. Though he liked wine, he knew nothing about making it when he started. He has shown that even an art as subtle and complicated as the making of good wine can be mastered by someone with enthusiasm, application and, of course, money. He has installed new vats and planted new vines. The proof of the wine is in the drinking, and Mr Ryman's white wine has won silver and bronze medals, and his red wine two gold medals at the great Mâcon Wine Fair. The charming old golden stone château was built by Henri IV of France for the star in his string of mistresses, Gabrielle d'Estrées.

For wine-tasting, telephone first: 53 58 32 11.

Most of the vineyards south of

the river are west of Monbazillac. The villages are small and, like those of the Double and the Landais, lie in gently undualting country. But here the subsoil is more porous, and the land is lower, and these factors result in an altogether more amiable countryside, varied and often very pretty. A pleasant drive can be made from Monbazillac via the **Moulin de Malfourat**, where there is a terrace with a good view over the Dordogne valley, to Pomport and then Sigoulès, a village responsible for a large production of AOC wines. A better than average red Bergerac is made at **Château Panisseau**, tucked away in deep countryside near the little River Besage, north of the road from Sigoulès to Thénac, and via a side turning to the right. Beyond Panisseau, the road leads to the village of **Cunèges**, where there is a small Romanesque church. From Cunèges, the D15 leads north of La Ferrière.

Keen walkers may like to know that the GR6, one of the *Grande Randonnée* national footpaths, crosses this stretch of countryside from west to east, and can be picked up at Gageac et Rouillac, just to the south of La Ferrière, or a little further to the west at **Saussignac**, another important wine-producing centre.

From Saussignac, a few miles on the D4 southwards brings you to the D18; and another 9 miles (15km) to the pleasant little *bastide* of **Eymet**, originally built in 1271 by Alphonse de Poitiers. The village square, with its arches and timbered houses,

still has an air of the Middle Ages. In the 14th-century *donjon*, all that remains of the castle, there is a small museum dedicated to local history and folklore. Eymet is famous for the production of *foie gras* from both goose and duck livers. If, instead of making for Eymet, you turn north on the D18, you come to **Ste-Foy-la-Grande**. This is another 13th-century *bastide*, on the banks of the Dordogne, still with its arcaded central square and a few old houses, but all now rather swamped by an unlovely agglomeration. There are one or two good restaurants in the old part of the town, notably **La Vieille Auberge**, 10 rue Louis Pasteur (tel: 57 46 04 78) and that of the **Grand Hôtel**, 117 rue de la République (tel: 57 46 00 08), which has a cheap menu for children.

Ste-Foy-la-Grande is on the south bank of the Dordogne, and is actually in Gironde; but the north bank is still Dordogne, and if you go west on the D936 for a few miles you come to a place called **Tête-Noire**, where a turning to the right leads to Montcaret and the chateau of Montaigne.

Tête-Noire is named from Geoffrey Tête-Noire, a famous captain of *routiers* during the Hundred Years War. *Routiers* was a polite name for freelance gangs of bandits or highwaymen, made up of disaffected soldiers and others, who thought that robbery was a better way of making a living than fighting other professionals. Tête-Noire and his men held up travellers to and from Bordeaux.

PÉRIGORD BLANC

BOURDEILLES
*6 miles (10km) southwest of
Brantôme, on the D78*
Here, a castle stands on a cliff
above the river and, below, the
village houses are grouped near
a 13th-century hump-backed
bridge, and the river burbles
past a picturesque fortified mill.
There are really two châteaux
on the rock at Bourdeilles: one
an unfinished Renaissance
palace, the other a massive
medieval fortress with walls
8 feet (2m) thick, the ancestral
home of the Bourdeille family. It
was here that Pierre de
Bourdeille was born in 1540
(see **Brantôme**, below).
Bourdeille was one of the four
baronies of Périgord, the others
being Biron, Beynac, and
Mareuil. The family is said to
have become prominent at the
time of the Crusades when,
according to legend, they
became famous as slayers of
griffins, a beast which in most
other places is regarded as an
entirely mythical cross between
a lion and an eagle. The
Bourdeilles are said to have
added to their reputation by
going far beyond Jerusalem to
slay a dragon and bring back
some holy oil which it had
hidden in its ear. That, as they
say, is as may be, but griffins do
feature in the arms of the
Bourdeille family, and the local
hotel is the Hostellerie des
Griffons.
The most impressive part of the
old castle is the 111-foot (34m)-
high keep, built as a defence
against English attacks during
the Hundred Years War. It has a
spiral staircase which leads to a

terrace at the top with splendid
views of the surrounding
countryside, but the climb
should be tackled only by those
sound in wind and limb.
According to Pierre de
Bourdeille, the unfinished
Renaissance palace adjoining
the medieval fortress was
designed by his sister-in-law,
Jaquette de Montbron, without
the help of an architect. She did
well. The building is impressive,
and on the first floor there is a
splendid Salon Doré (the
Golden Room) said to have
been created especially for a
visit from the Queen, Catherine
de Medici, a friend of the family.
But she never came, being too
occupied in fighting religious
and political enemies to visit
those whom she knew to be
loyal.
Open: daily, morning and
afternoon, 1 July to 7 September;
daily (except Tuesdays) outside
this time.

Accommodation
Down at the riverside next to the
lovely 13th-century bridge, the
Hostellerie des Griffons, Le
Pont, 24310 (tel: 53 03 75 61) is a
16th-century house completely
renovated a few years ago. It
has 10 comfortable bedrooms at
a little above average prices,
and a good restaurant.

BRANTÔME
*17 miles (27km) north of
Périgueux by the D939*
Brantôme is one of the most
attractive little towns in
Périgord. Much of it is on an
island enclosed by two arms of
the River Dronne, so that there

The island town of Brantôme, with its old abbey, on the River Dronne

are five bridges, including the 16th-century Pont Coude (Elbow Bridge), steeply arched to allow for possible floods. The old houses covered with creepers, the riverside gardens, the weeping willows, the tall bell tower of the abbey reflected in the river, the old streets, all combine to make Brantôme a pleasant place to wander in. The chief interest in Brantôme is the old **abbey** beside the Dronne. Believed to have been founded by Charlemagne in 769, when he deposited there some relics of St-Sicaire, one of Herod's slaves who had been converted to Christianity after the Massacre of the Holy Innocents, the abbey has frequently been restored. In the 19th century it was mauled about by an architect named Abadié, a man of great enthusiasm but considerably less judgement, who was also responsible for

the extraordinary restoration of the cathedral of St-Front in Périgueux, and who designed the Sacré Coeur in Paris. In Brantôme he succeeded in spoiling both the church and the cloister. The abbey, having been destroyed by the Normans, was rebuilt in the 11th century, and the bell tower erected at that time has somehow survived for 800 years and was one thing that Abadié left alone. The abbey and belltower are open all year, except Tuesdays 1 September to 30 June.

The abbey buildings, which have Renaissance pavilions at either end, as well as the bell tower, form an impressive group beside the river.

Both the abbey and the town are closely associated with the late 16th-century French writer Pierre de Bourdeille, who was the younger son of the High Sheriff of Périgord. The estates were inherited by his brother André, who became High Sheriff in his turn and married a rich and beautiful wife. Pierre was obliged to become a soldier and fought in Italy, Morocco and Malta, and later became a courtier to Catherine de Medici and her three sons, each of whom became in turn, and briefly, king of France. It was Pierre de Bourdeille's diplomatic skill which saved the abbey from destruction during the religious wars between Catholics and Huguenots.

His career was cut short in 1589, when at the age of 49 he fell from his horse. He was crippled and bed-ridden for four years, and for the remainder of his life he was condemned to physical inactivity and rest. But it was this accident which eventually brought him fame. He retired to Brantôme, took the name of the town as his pseudonym and put together books which were a mixture of society gossip and pornography, based on his long association with the great. His *Lives of Famous Men and Great Soldiers* and, more so, his *Lives of Amorous Ladies*, pulled no punches and were considered witty and entertaining, often because his cynical turn of mind never allowed the truth to get in the way of a good yarn. These books are still read today. Though he is much better known to posterity than the older brother he envied, Pierre de Bourdeille did not achieve literary fame in his own lifetime; but he prospered well enough to build himself the **Château de Richemont**, 4 miles (7km) from Brantôme by the D939 at St-Crepin de Richemont. This is where, after his accident,

he lived and worked, and eventually died, and he is buried in the chapel.

The château is open morning and afternoons, 15 July to 31 August, except on Fridays, Sunday mornings and the morning of 15 August.

Accommodation

There is first-class accommodation in the countryside near Brantôme. At Champagnac-de-Belair, 4 miles (6km) north of Brantôme on the route to Puyguilhem, the **Hostellerie du Moulin du Roc** (tel: 53 54 80 36) is very up-market. It is a very comfortable hotel in grounds with a swimming pool on the banks of the Dronne. The restaurant has a Michelin star and prices are high. The number of tables is limited, so reservations should be made. There is a lower price menu for children.

On a less exalted level, back in Brantôme itself, the **Auberge du Soir**, 24310 Brantôme (tel: 53 05 82 93) is a small hotel in the Logis de France group, and it is representative of the sound standards and economical prices offered by this type of hotel.

Just outside Brantôme, on the road to Bourdeilles, there is an attractive private hotel called **Le Chatenet**, route de Bourdeilles (tel: 53 05 81 08). This 18th-century country house stands in 10 acres (4 hectares) with gardens and swimming pool. There are only four bedrooms and three apartments. Breakfast is served, but there is no restaurant; but it is only a little way from those in Brantôme.

Restaurants

Brantôme is a good base for touring in Dordogne and has several hotels and restaurants. Those who like to offer themselves the good things of life while travelling are not likely to be disappointed by the rooms or the restaurant of the **Moulin de l'Abbaye**, 24310 Brantôme (tel: 53 03 80 22). The chef, Monsieur Ravinel, was for two years at the Troisgros in Roanne, one of France's greatest restaurants, and also worked in England at the well-known Waterside Inn at Bray on the Thames, near Windsor. A one-Michelin-star restaurant with standards and prices to match. Somewhat larger, somewhat cheaper, and with particularly good value in the restaurant, is the **Grand Hôtel Chabrol**, 57 rue Gambetta (tel: 53 05 70 15), equally well known in Dordogne as **Les Frères Charbonnel** (the brothers Charbonnel).

◆◆
CHÂTEAU DE MONTRÉAL

on the D38 from Mussidan to Issac

This privately owned castle dates from the 12th to the 16th centuries, and was the home of the Pontbriant family. Claude de Pontbriant, Seigneur de Montréal, was with Jacques Cartier when the famous explorer made his second voyage to the St-Lawrence River. On 3 October, 1535, Cartier named a small Indian settlement after his friend's property in Périgord. It was to become the second largest French-speaking town in the world, with over a million inhabitants today.

Another story associated with the Château de Montréal concerns La Chapelle de la Ste-Épine, which the Pontbriant family built on their property in

More homely than imposing...the Château de Montréal

1569 to house a thorn from the Crown of Thorns. This thorn is said to have been taken by one of their ancestors from the body of the English general, Sir John Talbot, killed at the battle of Castillon in 1453.

In any case, Montréal, with its medieval fortifications, its Renaissance residence and gracious chapel, is an attractive and interesting château.

Open: 1 July to 30 September, morning and afternoon.

PÉRIGORD BLANC

◆
FORÊT DE LA DOUBLE
west and southwest of Périgueux
This large tract of wild and
forested country is crossed by
only one main road from east to
west: the N89, leading
eventually to Bordeaux; and by
one less important road from
north to south: the D708, from
Ribérac to Ste-Foy-la-Grande.
North of the N89 lies the Forêt
de la Double. There has been a
forest here from time
immemorial. The Romans knew
it and avoided it. Its undulating
hills and clay subsoil made it a
country of streams, bogs,
marshes and countless pools
and lakes. Much of the water
was stagnant, and the few
people who lived there were
martyrs to malaria and other
swamp fevers. It was a district
where people went to hide and
risk disease rather than face
their enemies. The Double
(pronounced *doo-bler*)
remained for hundreds of years
a gloomy, sinister, unhealthy
place. Even now there are parts
of it that still seem dank and
uninviting, except in early
summer, when the countless
Spanish chestnut trees are
loaded with their spikes of
yellow blossom, or on sunny
days in high summer.
Things were much improved in
the late 19th century, when a
Trappist monastery was set up
near Echourgnac in the heart of
the forest. The monks drained
much of the forest, cleared the
land and cultivated crops.
Today, malaria is a thing of the
past and the larger lakes, such
as the Étang de la Jemaye, have
had their banks cleared and

sown with grass, and are now
centres for water sports. The
monastery is still there, and is
now called the **Abbaye
d'Echourgnac**, **Notre Dame
d'Espérance**, but the monks
have been replaced by nuns of
the same Trappist order. They
have a shop where they sell
their own produce. There are
also 24 guest rooms for visitors
who wish to go into retreat.
From this island of calm, with its
neat lawns and paths, there are
panoramic views over wild and
tangled forest.
The Forêt de la Double lies
between the River Dronne and
the River Isle.

◆
FORÊT DU LANDAIS
*south of the N89 from Mussidan
and between the River Isle and
the River Dordogne*
This is more open and less
watery than the Double. In the

Pines are still predominant in the once wild Forêt du Landais

19th century a pine forest was planted in the Landes department, south of Bordeaux, to hold back the encroaching sands, which were turning farm land to desert. A prosperous resin industry developed from these pines, and people looked for other places to plant pines from which to take the resin. Some chose this part of Périgord, and it became known as the Forêt du Landais. The resin industry is now dead, but there is still a high proportion of pines in this forest.

Both forest areas are still thinly populated, and their interest for the visitor lies in the scenery, the remoteness and the wildlife. The D709 leads through the Forêt du Landais down to Bergerac from Mussidan, which lies on a loop of the Isle between the Double and the Landais. **Mussidan** had a rough time during the Hundred Years War, when it was an important English strongpoint; and during the religous wars, when it was a Protestant base repeatedly attacked by the Catholics; and again during World War II, when it was sacked by the Germans, who turned out every house down to the last gold ring and the last bottle of wine, in retaliation for a Resistance attack on an armoured train. But this is a place which insists on being ordinary. 'Worth a detour' is not a phrase that comes to mind, though there is a museum to local art and traditions, open daily (except Tuesdays) June to September, and afternoons October to May. It is on a main road, and one can get a satisfactory lunch there, but rarely a memorable one.

◆
MONCARET
off the D936, west of Ste-Foy-la-Grande
Moncaret may not be an obvious tourist halt, but it is worth a visit for those interested in ancient history. It was a thriving village in Roman times, and has some Gallo-Roman remains, including excellent mosaics, among them a Roman bath decorated with fish and an octopus. There are also some tombs of Visigoths, and a good early Romanesque church. In the small museum there is a collection of pottery, coins, and other items found by archaeologists on the site.
St Michel de Montaigne, just down the road from Moncaret, is

PÉRIGORD BLANC

a dozy village, whose only interest is that it was here that France's great essayist, Michel de Montaigne, was born, lived and died. He was born in the château originally bought by his great-grandfather, Ramon Eyquem, a business man and wine merchant of Bordeaux, in 1477. Montaigne was the son of Pierre d'Eyquem and Antoinette de Louppes, or Lopez. She belonged to a rich Bordeaux family, which was of Jewish and Portuguese descent, and had emigrated from Spain to escape persecution.

Montaigne always had a strong sympathy for the peasants and their situation, and did not hesitate to express it. And in the essays which brought him such lasting distinction, his thought and language had the strength and clarity of the Latin writers he admired.

All that remains of the original château is the round tower, where Montaigne worked. It had two rooms: a library and a bedroom. On the ceiling beams of his library he had inscribed sayings from his favourite Latin authors, from which he could always draw inspiration. Archaeology was an unknown science in his day, and he could

Fine mosaics decorate the Roman remains at Moncaret

never have known that only a short stroll from where he worked, there lay under the ground positive evidence of the civilisation he so much admired. It is a curious fact that nothing is known of the fate of his 1,000 books. They were given by his only surviving daughter, Léonore, to the Abbé de Roquefort, but what happened to them later is a mystery.

The tower, with Montaigne's library, his bedroom, and, on the ground floor, a small chapel, is open to the public morning and afternoon, except Mondays and Tuesdays and early January to mid February. The rest of the château was burned down in the 19th century, and rebuilt by a Monsieur Magne, who was Minister of Finance during the Second Empire.

◆◆
PÉRIGUEUX
on the crossroads of the N21 (Limoges to Bergerac) and the N89 (Bordeaux to Clermont Ferrand); 29 miles (47km) north of Bergerac
Situated in the heart of the department of the Dordogne, of which it is the préfecture, Périgueux is an ideal base for the tourist who wants to see as much of the region as possible. It is feasible to make a different excursion every day and return to a good hotel and a wide choice of restaurants in the evening.

Périgueux is not a town to be judged on first impressions. The main routes through it suggest that it is of less than average prosperity and interest. But it is a place which improves a great deal on closer acquaintance, and especially for those visitors who are prepared to take their time on foot.

The town has a long and disturbed history. After the conquest of Gaul by Julius Caesar, it was converted from a simple Gaulish settlement into an important Roman town, and it has never again achieved the relative degree of prosperity, either in the Middle Ages or in modern times, that it enjoyed during the long Roman occupation.

Since Roman times it has been pillaged by barbarians, attacked and burned by the Normans, besieged by the English during the Hundred Years War, divided and damaged in the Wars of Religion, and suffered German oppression and occupation during World War II, because of the strength of the French Resistance movement in the area.

The Romans called their town Vesunna and the most important of the remains from that time is the **Tour de Vésone** (Vesunna Tower). It formed part of a temple built in the 2nd century AD, the 'golden age' of the Roman Empire. The tower is 78 feet (24m) high and a garden, with pieces of Roman statuary found during excavations, has been laid out around it.

The Roman town included a spa with public baths, an amphitheatre which could seat 20,000 people, well laid-out streets and luxury villas of prosperous merchants and officials. One of these villas, near the Tour de Vésone, has been excavated by archaeologists. It is believed to have belonged to a member of the family of Pompey, the great rival of Julius Caesar. The remains indicate the high standard of living enjoyed by well-to-do Romans nearly 2,000 years ago. The villa had three large reception rooms and 60 smaller rooms arranged around a colonnaded courtyard. The amenities included extensive kitchens and storerooms, central heating, shady galleries and fountain courts.

Of the Roman **amphitheatre** – one of the largest in Gaul – not much remains apart from the entrances and some of the great blocks of stone used in its construction. The central arena has been made into a public garden.

Part of the Roman wall of Vesunna can be seen. The **Château Barrière** is a fortified house built in the Middle Ages on this wall.

When the Roman Empire in the

Once part of a Roman temple, the Tour de Vésone now stands alone

west came to an end in the 4th century AD, Vesunna was abandoned. It was a Christian saint, St-Front, who began the revival of the town by establishing a church among the ruins, probably in the early 4th century. The old town lay within a great bend of the River Isle, but St-Front was buried on top

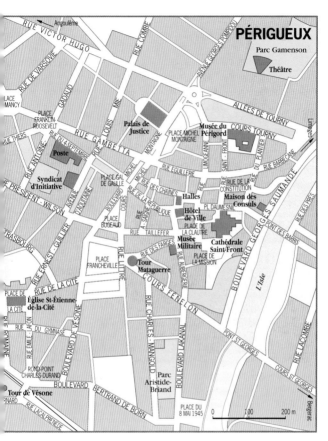

of a nearby hill (*puy*).
Pilgrimages were made to the
site, and gradually two towns
developed side by side. The
one in the bend of the river was
known as La Cité, and the one
on the hill as Puy St-Front.
There was long rivalry between
the two towns, each of which
was enclosed within its own
wall. Though they were officially
amalgamated into one town
called Périgueux in 1240, the

rivalry continued. During the
Hundred Years War the Cité
was loyal to England, and Puy
St-Front to France.
By the end of the Hundred Years
War battles and epidemics had
reduced the population of
Périgueux to less than 2,000.
It was not until the end of the
15th century that the town began
to revive, but the religious wars
of the 16th century brought
more troubles. The worst attack

The 'oriental' Cathédrale St-Front grew from a Roman town's ruins

was in 1575, when the Cathédrale St-Front was damaged by the Protestant army, the church treasure was taken, and the saint's tomb destroyed. Two years later, the church of St-Étienne de la Cité, in those days a cathedral, was badly damaged in another attack.

It was not until after the French Revolution, when Périgord was chosen as the administrative centre of the department, that the town began to become more important. In 1800 it had a population of 6,000, but by 1850 the figure had reached 13,000. The question that worried all town authorities in the middle of the 19th century was: would the railway come to them, or pass them by? Périgueux was lucky: the railway arrived in 1856. A few years later railway repair workshops were set up, and the renovation of rolling stock and the manufacture of rails and accessories for the French railway system is probably still the most important industry in the town.

Périgueux cannot be called an industrial town, but it does have more industry than anywhere

has been carried out in recent years. The chief points of interest are shown on a plan which can be obtained from the

else in Dordogne. All French postage stamps, so much admired by philatelists both for their design and the quality of the printing, are produced in Périgueux. There is a clothing industry, and a number of food manufacturers producing specialities such as *pâté de foie gras*. The town is also a headquarters for several departments of the French Civil Service.

Apart from the vestiges of Roman occupation in the Cité, interest for tourists is concentrated in the **old town**, around the Cathédrale St-Front, where a restoration programme

Truffles and *Foie Gras*

Despite many expensive efforts, the world famous Périgord black truffle, a member of the fungus family, has defied all attempts at commercial cultivation. As a consequence, it still has to be collected in the local oak forests, where, despite the stories, it is more likely to be sniffed out by a dog than a pig.

The truffle grows underground, the animals picking up the scent: pigs were once used as hunters, but their tendency to eat what they found – as opposed to dogs, who do not share the pig's partiality – means they have lost favour with collectors. The true Périgord truffle has to carry the label *truffes de Périgord*. When you see the price, you will not wonder that the truffle-eating pig is no longer the truffle-hunter's best friend.

A second Périgord speciality is *foie gras*, which translates as fat liver. The livers in question are from geese or ducks fed on a diet of partially cooked maize so that their body weight, and liver weight, increase dramatically.

As with the truffle, *foie gras* is strictly controlled. The connoisseur eats it almost raw, but most folk eat a paté or terrine which contains about 25% minced pork or veal. If the percentage rises to 50% then the law states that the word *gras* must be dropped from the food's title.

PÉRIGORD BLANC

Tourist Office (26 place Francheville). Among them are the **Maison de St-Front** (16th-century), on the corner of the rue de la Constitution and the rue Plantier; the **Maison Pâtissier** (1518), in the rue Eguillerie; and the **Maison des Dames de la Foi**, in the rue des Farges. There are many fine houses of the Renaissance period in the rue Limogeanne, the rue Barbecane, and beside the River Isle.

The **Cathédrale St-Front**, as a building, is nothing if not unusual. Its appearance is known to many people who have never been to Périgueux, as its oriental-looking domes and turrets are as much the trade-mark of Périgueux as the Eiffel Tower is of Paris. As it stands today, practically the whole of St-Front is 19th-century. The former building, dating from 1173, was so dilapidated that, when it was decided to restore it, the architect, Abadié, launched into a frenzy of rebuilding, adding 17

Renaissance houses crowd together near the river in Périgueux

turrets to the existing five domes, and a 196-foot (60m) belfry topped by a lantern tower and a conical spire. The overall effect is curious.

The interior of St-Front is spacious and lofty, but has little more religious feeling about it than an empty warehouse. Students of church architecture may well find it interesting, but most tourists are likely to prefer the view of it from across the river.

The **Musée du Périgord** is paticularly strong in its prehistory and Gallo-Roman collections. Much of the prehistory collection is made up from finds in Dordogne, but not all of it. In the 1950s, when the French explorer, Pierre-Dominique Gaisseau, crossed New Guinea on foot from south to north, his expedition came into contact with the last tribes on earth who had never seen a white man. He found them using stone age tools and weapons, and in the Périgord museum tools from the prehistoric sites around Les Eyzies can be compared with similar tools still in use in the Pacific until recent times. The museum is open daily, except Tuesdays.

In the Middle Ages Puy St-Front was fortified by 28 round towers. One of these still stands: the **Tour Mataguerre**, at the side of the place Francheville in the centre of the town.

In the second half of the 15th century, when Périgueux suffered from a severe epidemic of leprosy, the Tour Mataguerre was restored by a work force consisting entirely of lepers.

Accommodation

Hotels in town

Hôtel Domino, 21 place Francheville, Périgueux 2400 (tel: 53 08 25 80). A former posting inn, this is a pleasant and comfortable hotel, centrally situated. It has a flowery courtyard, used as an outside dining room in summer. The restaurant is good, and prices both for meals and rooms are a little above average.

Hôtel Ibis, 8 boulevard Georges-Saumonde-St-Front (tel: 53 53 64 58). The largest hotel in Périgueux with 89 rooms. One of a well-known chain of modern and moderately priced hotels. Nicely situated between the Cathédrale St-Front and the River Isle. Good but restricted restaurant menus; special price for children.

Hôtel du Périgord, 74 rue Victor Hugo (tel: 53 53 33 63).

Although in town, this hotel is a member of the Logis de France organisation, and offers representative standards and prices.

Hotels within easy reach of Périgueux

Hôtel les Chandelles, Antonne-et-Trigonant, 24420 Savignac-les-Églises (tel: 53 06 05 10). Six miles (10km) northeast of Périgueux by N21. A charming, small hotel (seven bedrooms) in a converted 15th-century building beside the river. Tennis and fishing. Good restaurant with special rate for children.

Hôtel le Lion d'Or, place de l'Église, Manzac-sur-Vern, 24110 St-Astier (tel: 53 54 28 09). A charming little village hotel, a Logis de France, with a restaurant strong on regional dishes. Manzac is reached from Périgueux, about 6 miles (10km), by the N21 going south, and then right on to the D4.

Hôtel le Parc, Savignac-les-Églises, 24270 Lanouailles (tel: 53 05 08 11). A pleasant, recently modernised hotel, with swimming pool in the grounds. Prices are above average, but as it is close to a hotel school, the high standards are likely to be maintained. Reached from Périgord by the N21 going north and then the D705.

Hôtel le St-Laurent, St-Laurent-sur-Manoire, 24330 St-Pierre de Chignac (tel: 53 04 28 28). Five and a half miles (9km) south of Périgueux by the N89, the Cahors road. A nice modern hotel, 48 rooms at average prices, placed in spacious grounds with swimming pool and tennis.

Restaurants

Périgueux is a show-place of the famous cuisine Périgourdine. Among the restaurants where you can try the specialities are **La Flambée**, rue Montaigne (tel: 53 53 23 06); **L'Oison**, 31 rue St-Front (tel: 53 09 84 02), a small restaurant where it is advisable to book in advance, as it is probably the best in Périgueux and proportionately expensive; **Le Retro**, 7 cours Fénelon (tel: 53 08 54 06), a pleasant bistro, reasonable prices; and the **Tournepiche**, 2 rue Nation (tel: 53 08 90 76), which has an 18th-century dining room. **Marcel**, 37 avenue Limoges (tel: 53 53 13 43), is a moderately priced, sound restaurant but closed in high season from about 25 July to 10 August. Cheaper for children.

◆
RIBÉRAC
on the D103 or the D710 (along the Dronne Valley)
Ribérac is an old town which has preserved little of its past. The castle which once protected it no longer exists. There is little of

Dining in Périgueux offers the chance to try good local dishes

interest in its old church, and less in the more modern one. It had some good medieval houses, but they were pulled down when streets were widened in the 19th century. Ribérac stands at a point where several routes meet to cross the Dronne and is a natural market town for a wide area of Périgord Blanc. On Friday mornings most of the town becomes a market place, with chickens and ducks in one square, fresh fruit and vegetables in another, household goods over here and rabbits and pigeons over there. It's a colourful scene, and with so much good produce at hand it is not surprising that the restaurant of the **Hôtel de France** can be recommended. A cross-country drive from Ribérac by the D709 to the south, and then the D45 by wooded hills to St-Aquilin and St-Astier on the Isle, and then the N89 to Périgueux, gives a good impression of the countryside of Périgord Blanc.

PÉRIGORD NOIR
(BLACK PÉRIGORD)

The whole of Périgord is rich in
scenic attractions and historical
interest, but, without doubt, it is
the region east of Bergerac and
on both sides of the Dordogne
which has the most
spectacularly sited castles, the
loveliest scenery, and a
uniquely interesting past.

WHAT TO SEE

BEAUMONT
on the D660
This is a *bastide* founded by the
English in 1272, and it is unusual
in that it takes the shape of an 'H'
instead of a rectangle,
supposedly in honour of Henry
III, who died that year. Its chief
interest today is its unusual
fortified church, which has
square towers at each corner. It
was built in the 13th and 14th
centuries, and was almost a ruin
when it was completely restored
in the 19th century. Guided
tours of the *bastide* operate
during July and August:
information from the Syndicat
d'Initiative.

Restaurants
Beaumont is a well-known lunch
stop for visitors touring the local
bastides. Two places are
especially popular: the **Hôtel
des Voyageurs**, 24440
Beaumont de Périgord, has a
few simple and modestly priced
rooms, and an unusual
restaurant well known all over
southern Dordogne. **Chez
Popaul** (tel: 53 22 30 11) calls
for a hearty appetite. On most of

its menus the second course
consists of an unlimited choice
from a selection of 40 *hors
d'oeuvres*. It should be
remembered that other courses

*Even the church is fortified in
Beaumont, built to outlast wars*

are still to follow! Prices are
moderate, but in the summer
season it is essential to book in
advance.

BEYNAC-ET-CAZENAC ✓

*on the D703, 2 miles (3km) from
La Roque-Gageac*
Beynac-et-Cazenac climbs a
cliff, and above it stands one of
the most dramatically sited
castles in Périgord. On foot, the
castle is an energetic climb from
the village. By car, it has to be
reached by a road that sweeps
inland for a couple of miles, and

then back to the castle. There is a charge for parking, whether you visit the castle or not.

Few places can give a visitor a stronger sense of the medieval past than this **Château de Beynac**, towering above a few houses humbly clinging to its skirts. There is no need to go into the castle in order to feel yourself transported back nearly a thousand years. It is possible to walk round to a viewpoint on top of the cliff, and to stand where Richard the Lionheart and his ruthless captain, Mercadier, stood when they had captured the original 12th-century fortress – today's castle was built one hundred years later by the Barons of Beynac – and were deciding how best to use this strongpoint to control the Dordogne valley. Mercadier was a very cruel man. At Beynac, he so terrorised the surrounding countryside that the castle was called 'the house of Satan'.

The village below the castle is explored along the steep Carnival del Panieraires, the basket-makers' path, which passes beautiful Renaissance houses, a museum dedicated to Beynac's Gallic history, and an archaeological park where scenes from the area's past – from Neolithic to Gallic times – are reconstructed.

Open: daily, in July and August, morning and afternoon, 1 March to 15 November.

Accommodation

Hôtel Bonnet, 24220 St-Cyprien (tel: 53 29 50 01). Old-established family hotel at river level.

Feudal power is embodied in the castle looming over Beynac

◆◆◆
BIRON ✓

5 miles (8km) south of Monpazier

The picturesque village of Biron is dominated by its huge castle which, from its hilltop, lords it over the surrounding countryside for 18 miles (30km) in every direction. The château, which belonged to the de Gontaut Biron family for nearly 800 years, is currently being expensively restored. It was built at the end of the 12th

century, and, as their fortunes prospered, 14 generations of the family, the premier barons of Périgord, added to the stronghold. It now consists of a dozen different buildings of varying architectural styles: Gothic arches here, Renaissance windows there, turrets and towers, and who knows what around the next corner.

In all this variety, the thing that says most about the Biron family is the unique double-naved chapel. Their self-esteem was so great that they felt they should have a private place of worship nearer to God than that of the ordinary people. So they built on top of the existing parish church, creating a building in which their family chapel could be entered from the castle courtyard, while the villagers continued to use the church beneath the Biron feet.

There are fine views from the castle terraces and among the many interesting things in the interior are the Renaissance apartments, and the largest vaulted kitchens in France.

Open: morning and afternoon throughout the year; closed 15 December to 31 January, and on Tuesdays outside the period from 1 July to 7 September.

PÉRIGORD NOIR

◆◆
CADOUIN

*on the D25 10 miles (16km)
northeast of Beaumont*

The former Cistercian Abbey of
Cadouin was founded in 1115. A
few years later the Bishop of Le
Puy, Adhemar de Monteil,
returned from a Crusade with a
piece of cloth from a church in
Antioch, which was said to have
bound the head of Christ at the
Crucifixion. This relic attracted
pilgrims to Cadouin and made
the abbey famous and
prosperous for hundreds of
years. Countless pilgrims on
their way to St-James of
Compostella halted at Cadouin
to revere this piece of cloth.
Eleanor of Aquitaine, Richard
the Lionheart, St-Louis and
Charles V, and many more of
the great and famous also came
to kneel before it. But since the
1930s there have been no more
pilgrimages to Cadouin,
because at that time experts
established that the Kufic
(Arabic) inscriptions
embroidered on the cloth could
not be earlier than the 11th
century. In other words, the
cloth was new when given to the
abbey.
But Cadouin is still well worth
visiting. It is one of the best
preserved abbeys of France.
The original abbey church,
consecrated in 1154, is simple to
the point of severity, but its
bareness serves to emphasise
the harmony of the Romanesque
construction. By contrast with its
early simplicity, Cadouin has a
superb cloister in the
Flamboyant Gothic style. Work
on the cloister started at the end
of the 15th century and

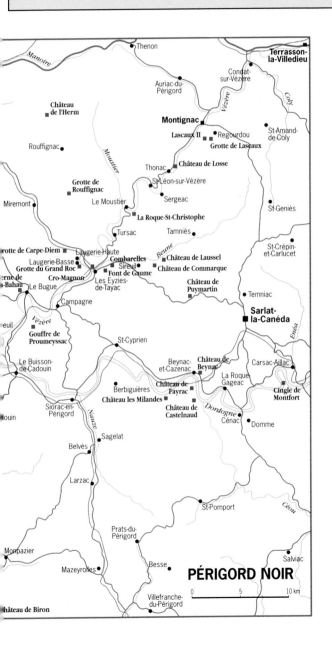

PÉRIGORD NOIR

continued for 50 years, the new cloisters replacing those ruined during the Hundred Years War.

Cadouin's renowned Cistercian Abbey, which has an impressive Flamboyant Gothic cloister

Although some of the fine sculpture is now in poor condition or has been effaced – it is said that one of the abbots disapproved of the levity with which the sculptor had treated some themes – there are still many fine examples of late Gothic and early Renaissance carving in the capitals and in the details of the vaulting.

Open: morning and afternoon throughout the year, but closed from 15 December to 31 January. Also within the village is one of France's best bicycle museums, with over 100 models, including one from the very first Tour de France, in 1903.

Open: daily throughout the year.

◆◆
CASTELNAUD AND FAYRAC
2½ miles (4km) south of Beynac, on the other side of the Dordogne
The charming château of Fayrac was originally a 13th-century fortress, but is now mostly a 15th- and 16th-century building, carefully restored and improved over the years. It is privately owned, and not open to the public.

Close by, but higher up, stands the **fortress of Castelnaud** (not to be confused with the Château de Castelnau, without a 'd', which overlooks the confluence of the Dordogne and the Céré in the Lot department). This castle was the great rival of Beynac during the Hundred Years War, when the Caumont family, who had become seigneurs of Castelnaud by marriage in 1368, took the side of the English. The French, based in Beynac, repeatedly attacked Castelnaud and finally captured it in 1442. Ten years after the end of the Hundred Years War, Louis XI forgave the Caumonts for having supported the English and gave them back Castelnaud in 1463. They fortified and enlarged it, but when François de Caumont married, his young wife thought Castelnaud too grim for a home. To please her he built the more gracious and habitable Château les Milandes, a few miles away, and surrounded it with gardens and terraces, and went to live there in 1489 (see page 64).

During the Wars of Religion, Castelnaud was used as a base by Geoffroy de Vivans, an officer in the Protestant army who had been born there, and during this period the fortifications were increased. During the 18th century the Caumonts ceased to maintain this castle, and at the time of the Revolution it was abandoned,

and gradually fell to ruin.
An important restoration of the castle was started in 1967. The keep and some parts have been renovated and re-roofed, and the castle now houses an interesting museum of medieval warfare, with full size reproductions of various war machines in use then.
There are panoramic views of the Dordogne valley from the terrace.
Open: daily, April to November.

Houses cluster around Castelnaud fortress, once the rival of Beynac

◆
CHÂTEAU DE COMMARQUE
along GR6 national footpath from Sireuil
The Château de Commarque, near Sireuil, part of the commune of Les Eyzies, is certainly one of the most photogenic ruins in the whole region. This great 12th-century castle was enclosed by a double ring of ramparts, the first of which protected a village now ruined and invaded by the forest. The elegant ruins of an ancient chapel can still be seen above the gateway in this outer wall.

Higher up, a second rampart surrounds the ruined castle, protected once by a guard-house, now crumbled and with tall trees growing within its walls. The tall keep, part 12th- and part 14th-century, still stands, with a cliff edge on one side and a deep ditch on the other. In the keep a spiral staircase leads to a terrace in the battlements, from which there are splendid views. The rugged and grandiose nature of these ruins can be compared with the view of the charming little château of Laussel (not open to the public), just across the valley of the Beune.

All the old castles in Dordogne played their part in the Hundred Years War, and Commarque changed hands several times during the hostilities, and was heavily damaged.

◆

CHÂTEAU DE LANQUAIS
south of Couze, off the D37
The Château de Lanquais is a 14th-century Gothic castle, to which has been added a late 16th-century palace. This extension was by Galiot de la Tour d'Auvergne, member of a family who played a major part in the history of France over 300 years. A long succession of cardinals, bishops, dukes, counts, generals and admirals from the Tour d'Auvergne family devoted their lives to the service of France. The women became the mistresses, wives and mothers of the great. One of them, Madeleine de la Tour, was mother of Catherine de Medici. Catherine ruled during the Wars of Religion. She assembled a group of beautiful and noble young ladies, whose work it was to 'charm and influence' powerful Protestants, without themselves being seduced. One of these women, who were popularly called Catherine's 'flying squadron', was Isabel de Limeuil, the sister of Galiot de la Tour d'Auvergne. When she was not at court, her home was the Château de Lanquais. Isabel was 'assigned' to work on the great Protestant leader, the Prince de Condé, but she had a child by him, whereupon Catherine 'sacked' her. The Prince de Condé is said to have accepted graciously his child, sent to him by Isabel in a basket. He died not long after, poisoned by his wife.

The Protestants besieged Lanquais in 1577 and the walls still show bullet marks from this attack. The interior has some beautiful chimney pieces and fine furniture. The château now belongs to a distinguished Bordeaux family, one of whose ancestors took Florida from the Spaniards in 1568. In the grounds a large barn – a Protestant church in the 16th century – is used in summer for concerts and exhibitions.
Open: daily, 1 July to 30 September; weekends in October; closed Thursdays, except July and August.

◆

CHÂTEAU DE LOSSE
3 miles (5km) from Montignac by the D706
The picturesque Château de Losse is attractively situated on a low cliff immediately above

The Château de Losse, once protected by moats, now welcomes visitors

the Vézère. On its other three sides it is surrounded by dry moats, and the entrance is a fortified gateway courtyard of the 14th century. The living quarters are in an L-shaped Renaissance building of later date, and there is a fine terrace overlooking the river. The château was the headquarters of Jean II of Losse, governor of Guyenne at the time of Henri IV. It has some very good period furniture and tapestries contemporary with its completion in the late 16th century. Privately owned.
Open: guided tours morning and afternoon 1 July to 30 September.

◆◆
CHÂTEAU DE PUYMARTIN
on the D47 from Sireuil towards Sarlat
The Château de Puymartin was rebuilt on earlier ruins in the 15th and 16th centuries by the St-Clar family, and then passed into the hands of the de Marzacs, who have owned it for 500 years. The château, built in the golden stone of Périgord, was restored during the 19th century. There are attractive rooms with fine furniture from the 14th to 18th centuries and splendid tapestries, including some 18th-century Aubusson, and six old Flemish tapestries showing scenes from the Trojan War, plus some curious paintings on the wooden panelling. But it does not have the museum atmosphere of so many great houses kept open for show. Fine as they are, the rooms at Puymartin have an atmosphere of ease found only in houses that have been continuously inhabited for a long time.
Open: guided tours mornings and afternoons, mid-April to mid-October.

◆◆
CHÂTEAU LES MILANDES

*2¹/₂ miles (4km) west of
Castelnaud, on D53*

This attractive château was
owned by the Caumont family
and retained by them until the
Revolution. Les Milandes was
very much restored during the
19th century, and is in a good
state of preservation today. After
World War II it was bought by
the famous star of the Folies
Bergères, Josephine Baker.
At the height of her fame and
fortune she always remembered
her rough childhood in St-Louis,

*The magnificent Château de
Puymartin has been home to the de
Marzac family for centuries*

Missouri, and when the war was
over she bought the Château les
Milandes, not as a luxury for
herself, but to provide a home
for children of different races,
colours, and religions, where
they could live in harmony. She
retired from the stage and spent
all her time and money on the
children, renovating the château
and creating a leisure park. It
was all too much. In 1964 she
was obliged to sell everything

and return to the stage to pay her debts. She died, shortly after her return, on the eve of a first night at a Paris theatre. The Château les Milandes is full of interest, with possessions and furniture associated with both the Caumont family and Josephine Baker. The reception rooms have some very fine carved woodwork, and the late 15th-century chapel, in Flamboyant Gothic style, is one of the finest in Dordogne. The style and the high quality of the stone carving suggest that it may have been the work of the same masons as those who built the magnificent cloisters of the Abbey of Cadouin.

Open: guided tours morning and afternoon, Palm Sunday to the end of September.

◆◆◆
DOMME ✓

6 miles (10km) south of Sarlat by the D46

Domme is a magnificently situated *bastide* village which gets more popular and more crowded every summer. The great craggy cliff of Domme, overlooking a wide area of the river valley and the surrounding countryside, was an obvious site, and the *bastide* was built by the French in 1281. The majority of *bastides* are plain rectangles, but Domme differs in being narrow at the cliff edge and wider away from it, a trapezoidal shape dictated by the slopes of the ground on which it was built.

Today, Domme still has most of its walls, and three fortified gateways.

Bastides

The Dordogne is superb country for the castle lover. *Bastides* – the word derives from the Occitan word *bastidas* – are a very special form of fortress which, while not unique to the Dordogne, reached their zenith here. The construction of *bastides* began in the 13th century, the first being the work of the Counts of Toulouse. They were new towns, usually built on hill tops which themselves offered protection from an invading force. The towns were laid out on a regular grid pattern, with encircling walls and defensive towers, sometimes even with a castle for further protection. In the Dordogne the best preserved *bastides* are at Domme and Monpazier.

It was such a natural fortress position that, over the years, its inhabitants began to regard it as impregnable. But in the 16th-century religious wars, the Protestant captain, Geoffroy de Vivans, a soldier of remarkable tenacity, courage and ingenuity, attacked it three times. In 1572 and 1577 he failed, but he had been born in the nearby castle of Fayrac, and had known Domme since his childhood, and in 1588 he decided to attempt what the residents of Domme thought was impossible. He assembled 30 picked men at the bottom of the cliff, and told the rest of his force to wait in complete silence outside the gates. Using coats to muffle the sound of their progress, he led his men laboriously up the face of the cliff, resting halfway in a cave. Once at the top, they crept to the middle of the town and then created an uproar, shouting, beating drums and clashing their weapons. Before the confused inhabitants, roused from sleep, could gather their wits, de Vivans' men had opened the gates and let in more attackers, and Domme was captured with hardly a blow struck. De Vivans' morals did not reach the same high level as his military skill. He was a professional, a mercenary, and four years later, in 1592, he sold Domme to the Catholics for 40,000 livres, a fortune in those times.

Domme is a well-restored village, with many attractive houses solidly built in the local yellow stone. The most impressive of these, the 16th-century **Maison du Gouverneur** (Governor's House), in the market square, has a tower with corner turrets, and looks solid enough to stand for hundreds more years.

Of the three fortified gateways, the most interesting is the **Porte des Tours**. The Porte gateway, including the prison of the Knights Templars, is open to the public (afternoons only), all year.

The factor which led to the building of Domme, its commanding clifftop position, is still its greatest attraction. The belvedere, called La Barre, looks out on the poplar-lined Dordogne far below, dotted in summer with different coloured canoes, and away to the left can be seen the village of La Roque-Gageac against its cliff. In front, beyond the valley, the hills roll away and climb

Domme is a well-restored and attractive example of the purpose-built bastides, *medieval reminders of a constantly warring age*

towards the Massif Central, altogether one of the finest panoramas in the whole of Dordogne.

The present day inhabitants of Domme have gone to some trouble to beautify their houses with pots of flowers and climbing plants, and it is certainly a well-restored and pretty place. But Domme, in common with Sarlat and a number of other picturesque small towns and villages throughout France, is becoming drowned in a fairground bazaar atmosphere very much at odds with its true historical character. In Domme, almost every house in the main street is a café or shop, with its tables or products spilling out into the street. There is a complex of caves in the rock beneath the village, in which the people used to hide when Domme was under attack in the Hundred Years War and the Wars of Religion. They contain stalactites and other crystalline formations of moderate interest, and they extend under the whole village. The entrance to the caves is below the covered market (*halle*): the caves are known locally as the *Grottes de la Halle* (*open*: 1 April to 31 October, mornings and afternoons).

The village of **Cénac**, at the riverside below Domme, has a church which still has its 12th-century chevet, though the rest of the building was completely restored during the 19th century. The capitals of the columns in the interior have some interesting carvings of animals.

Accommodation

The **Hôtel de L'Esplanade**, place de la Barre (tel: 53 28 31 41), at the corner of the belvedere, has a very pleasant terrace and a first-class restaurant, with windows with lovely views over the valley. The restaurant is moderately expensive but maintains standards very well from year to year. Rooms are comfortable and well furnished.

LES EYZIES-DE-TAYAC
on the D706, at the confluence of the River Beune and the River Vézère

Anyone who wants to voyage a little way into what has been called 'the night of time' should begin with a visit to the **Musée Nationale de Préhistoire** (National Museum of Prehistory), installed in the restored castle, once belonging to the Barons of Beynac, on the rock above the village of Les Eyzies.

This is no museum of musty rooms and dusty showcases. It has been updated and altered several times since its opening in 1923, and its clear arrangement enables visitors to form an idea of the chronology of the distant past. The earliest men shared the forests of Dordogne with mammoths and elephants, the rivers with the hippopotamus. Later, as the climate became colder, came reindeer, bear and the hairy rhinoceros, and later still tarpan horses, wild boar and bison. The museum makes all this clear, and also gives a basis for comparison of the cave paintings in different grottoes (see pages 69–72).

Museum open daily, except Tuesdays.

Les Eyzies is known as the capital of prehistory, because the first important discoveries were made there. The village, under a cliff resembling a Neanderthal's brow, is a somewhat uninspiring place, and suggests little of the fascination of the Vézère valley and its environs. But it makes a good base and has several hotels and restaurants.

There are something like 30 prehistoric sites in and around the Vézère valley, a few of which are listed below. There are also châteaux, ancient churches and picturesque villages worth visiting, as well as the ancient town of Sarlat with its many Renaissance buildings (see page 78).

Accommodation in or near Les Eyzies

There is always a strong demand for accommodation in Les Eyzies during July, August, and September, and it is better to telephone well in advance, especially if you have a particular hotel in mind.

Hôtel de Centenaire, 24620 Les Eyzies-de-Tayac (tel: 53 06 97 18). Opened in 1963, when Les Eyzies celebrated the centenary of the discovery of the first prehistoric sites, this is a hotel of above average comfort, with an exceptionally good restaurant. Rooms and meals are expensive. Within its own small grounds but at the junction of two main roads. Closed early November to 1 April.

Hôtel Cro-Magnon, route de Périgueux (tel: 53 06 97 06). Good example of the best type of traditional French family hotel, set in calm situation with 5 acres (2 hectares) of grounds. Superb restaurant with excellent wine list, and a spacious shady terrace for summer days. Comfortable rooms furnished in the old style, either in the hotel, or in an annexe in a quiet corner of the park. It's a very likeable hotel; not cheap but reasonable for what it offers.

Hôtel Les Glycines, route de Périgueux (tel: 53 06 97 07). A long-established and good hotel, not far from the village on the Périgord road, and set in pleasant grounds beside the Vézère. A sound hotel with a reasonably priced restaurant.

Hôtel Moulin de la Beune, route de Sarlat (tel: 53 06 94 33). A pleasant, moderately priced hotel beside the River Beune. It is not far from the main road, but some way below it, so that from the side of the road you look down to the hotel.

Le Bugue

This little town, about 6 miles (10km) from Les Eyzies by the D706, is an alternative base for exploring Black Périgord.

Hôtel du Château, Campagne, 24260 Le Bugue (tel: 53 07 23 50). Situated in the village of Campagne, about halfway between Le Bugue and Les Eyzies; D703 from Le Bugue, D706 from Les Eyzies. This is a pleasant, modern hotel, built in traditional style, with a first-class restaurant. Remarkable value at the prices asked. Closed November to Palm Sunday.

Hôtel Royal Vézère, place Hôtel de Ville, 24260 Le Bugue (tel: 53 07 20 01). A comfortable and

*Huddling beneath a limestone cliff,
Les Eyzies-de-Tayac offers glimpses
of prehistoric life*

moderately expensive hotel,
beautifully sited beside the
Vézère, with swimming pool
and terrace on the roof, and two
restaurants. L'Albuca offers
Périgord cuisine of high
standard in a classical French
restaurant décor, and Le Jardin
de l'Albuca offers a much
simpler and considerably
cheaper menu. Hotel closed
October to April.

◆

GROTTE DE CARPE-DIEM
In addition to painted caves
there are, in the Les Eyzies area,
a number of impressive caves
with stalactite and stalagmite
formations. One of these, the
Grotte de Carpe-Diem, near
Manaurie, can be seen on the
way to or from the Grotte de
Rouffignac. It has been
artistically lit to make the most of
the stalactites.

The cave is 2½ miles (4km)
north of Les Eyzies by the D47,
and a few hundred yards down
a side turning to the left.
Open: morning and afternoon,
Palm Sunday to 11 November.

◆

GROTTE DE COMBARELLES
*on the D47 towards Sarlat from
Les Eyzies*
The Grotte de Combarelles is a
treasure house of Magdalenien
art. There are about 300
drawings and paintings of
horses, bears, bison, reindeer
and mammoths, as well as
rhinoceros, wild cats, and the
usual mysterious designs. There
are also a number of human
profiles. Only about 100 visitors
are allowed each day, so you
must buy tickets in advance
from 09.00hrs for the morning
session and 14.00hrs for the
afternoon. The cave is open
morning and afternoon, and
closed on Wednesdays and
public holidays.

PÉRIGORD NOIR

◆
GROTTE DE FONT DE GAUME
*near junction of D48 to
St-Cyprien with D47 to Sarlat*
Here, in a long corridor cave
with side passages, you can see
some hundreds of paintings of
the Magdalenien period. They
include horses, bison,
mammoth, reindeer, and even a
rhinoceros and a wolf, all done
in very accomplished style, and
accompanied by the usual
'magic' symbols and signs.
This particular cave, only half a
mile (1km) from Les Eyzies, has
been known since the 18th
century, a time when nobody
attached any importance to
prehistoric art. Many of the
drawings were fading
noticeably, and there has been a
recent 'cleaning and restoration'
programme to freshen them up.
Visitor numbers are restricted in
high season and tickets must be
bought at about 09.00hrs.
Open: morning and afternoon,
except Tuesdays and public
holidays.

◆◆
GROTTE DU GRAND ROC
In the same area as the Grotte
de Carpe-Diem (see page 69) is
the Grotte du Grand Roc, a cave
with strange rock and crystal
formations, situated halfway up
an imposing cliff. From the steps
leading to the entrance, and
from the terrace in front of it,
there is a fine panorama of the
Vézère Valley.
The cave itself contains a
number of unusual crystalline
and coral-like formations, as
well as numerous stalactites and
stalagmites.
Open: daily, all year.

◆◆◆
GROTTE DE LASCAUX II ✓
1 mile (2km) south of Montignac
Although the original Lascaux
has been closed for more than
20 years, it has been possible
since 1983 for visitors to see
wonderful copies of its
paintings, and in almost
identical surroundings. A
nearby cave was remodelled,
using modern materials, to
conform exactly to the size and
shape of the main 'Bull
Chamber' of Lascaux I and the
adjoining Painted Gallery. On its
walls the paintings have been
reproduced exactly by artists
using the same methods as
prehistoric man.
They were helped by
photographs and computer
calculations, and in some cases
even used pigments from the
Magdalenien age, which had
been found in a nearby
gisement at Regourdou.
In the July/August high season,
entrance to Lascaux II is by
ticket, which can be bought only
at a special ticket office in
Montignac (see page 76). No
tickets are available at the site
itself. Groups are limited to 40
people at a time. Tickets are
stamped for a particular time of
day and are valid only for that
time. This system avoids the
hours of queueing that would
otherwise occur. Provided that
you arrive five minutes before
the time stamped on your ticket,
you will not have to wait. At the
ticket office in Montignac
(under the arcades of the
Syndicat d'Initiative) you may
buy a ticket for the next
available group, or for any later

Early television? Images of the hunt on display on the walls of the Grotte de Font de Gaume

time that suits you. Tickets are on sale from 09.00hrs.
Open: July and August, all day 09.30–19.30hrs; 1 February to 30 June and 1 September to 31 December, 10.00hrs–noon

and 14.00–17.30hrs. Tickets in high season are available only in Montignac, and out of season at the site.

◆
GROTTE DE ROUFFIGNAC
5 miles (8km) north of Les Eyzies
There are about 5 miles (8km) of galleries in this cave system, which has been known since the 15th century but was not fully explored until about 30 years ago.
A small electric train carries visitors through the most important parts of the cave.
There are engravings as well as paintings, including horses, ibex, rhinoceros, and so many

Caves and Cave Art
Dordogne has some huge and beautiful cave systems, one of the finest being the Gouffre de Padirac. Others gave shelter to early man, his artwork on the cavern walls being as beautiful as the flowstone formations. Of this art, the paintings at Lascaux are the best known, but those at Pech Merle – to the south of Rocamadour and just outside the area covered by this book – are equally beautiful, while the engravings at Rouffignac and Combarelles reveal an equally impressive talent.

mammoths that it is sometimes called 'the cave of the mammoths'. There is also a fine frieze of two stags fighting.

The vast cave is reached by the D47 north from Les Eyzies for about 6 miles (10km) to the hamlet of Miremont, where the D32 turns off to the right towards Rouffignac village. After about 3 miles (5km), another turning to the right (about 2 miles (3km) before the village itself) leads past an isolated farmhouse to the Grotte de Rouffignac.

Open: April to October, mornings 10.00–11.30hrs, afternoons 14.00–17.00hrs, opening an hour earlier and closing an hour later in July and August. The tour (minimum 20 people) takes an hour and it is advisable to take a pullover.

There are other things to see in and around Les Eyzies apart from painted caves and natural grottoes.

Near the station, in the part of the town called Tayac, there is a good example of a **fortified church**, dating from the 11th and 12th centuries.

Close to the Grotte du Grand Roc there is a **Museum of Speleology**, which will be of interest to pot-holers and cavers. (*Open*: daily, mid-June to mid-September.)

Animals of similar species to those drawn by prehistoric man can be seen in the park museum of **Centre d'Art Préhistorique du Thot** at Thonac, not far from Lascaux II. People buying a ticket for Lascaux II in the high season are given a complimentary ticket for Le Thot, which they can use as and

when they wish. The animals to be seen include European bison, Przewalski horses, red deer, fallow deer and onager (wild ass), and there are life-size robot mammoths and woolly rhinoceros, too. Le Thot has displays explaining the chronology and environment of prehistoric man, and an audio-visual introduction to cave art. The various stages in the construction of Lascaux II are also explained. Altogether it gives a clear introduction to prehistory which even young children can enjoy. Opening hours are the same as for Lascaux II (see page 70).

◆

LAUGERIE BASSE AND LAUGERIE HAUTE

2 miles (3km) north of Les Eyzies-de-Tayac, on D47

Man learned to read and write only a few thousand years ago; but he lived in Dordogne for not less than 150,000 years before that. Some aspects of the social history of those countless thousands of years have been interpreted through the examination of what generation after generation left behind: the bones of the animals they lived on, their own bones, their tools, weapons, utensils and ornaments. These remains have been, and are still being found at sites which had been continuously inhabited for thousands of years. They are known as *gisements*. Among the best known are those at *Laugerie Basse* and *Laugerie Haute*, a few miles from Les Eyzies-de-Tayac (see page 67–8). Laugerie Basse was continuously inhabited for at least 40,000 years, and until the advent of tourism was still inhabited by peasants. A late Victorian book has a drawing which illustrates a peasant's home there, as it was in the 1890s. It shows a room with an earth floor, a ceiling formed by the overhang of the natural rock, and the open side of this cliff shelter closed in by a roughly made wall with one unglazed window. The only furniture consists of a rough wooden table with two wooden benches, and a few baskets.

Hardly a setting for almost miraculous revelations. But the peasant who lived in that room, a Monsieur del Peyra, allowed a French archaeologist, whom he no doubt considered to be completely off his head, to dig a hole in the floor beside his bed. The archaeologist, Monsieur Massenat, went down 40 feet (12m) and cut through history. The first scientific investigations of prehistory in Dordogne had been made a few years earlier, in the 1860s, by another French archaeologist, Edouard Larter, and his friend, Henry Christy. These and other subsequent investigations at Laugerie have brought to light more than 500 objects, which, between them, cover a period from the Iron Age, more than a thousand years before Christ, back to the last Ice Age, 40,000 years ago, when man lived chiefly by hunting reindeer. Some of the finds are well arranged in a small

The fortified church of Les Eyzies-de-Tayac

museum at the site; others have been sent to museums all over France. They include harpoons, needles, engraved bones and stones, flints, arrow heads, lamps and pottery. There are still places in the Dordogne where such things may, by sheer luck, be found. These two sites illustrate mankind's long and continuous association with this part of Dordogne. But there are many other interesting prehistoric sites in the valley of the Vézère between Les Eyzies and Montignac (see pages 67 and 76) and in adjacent valleys. There are really too many to be seen, even systematically, in one average visit. A choice must somehow be made.

◆

LIMEUIL

at the confluence of the River Vézère and the River Dordogne (D51 from Le Buisson)
This is a very old village, beautifully sited on a hill overlooking the rivers Dordogne and Vézère, crossed by an elbow bridge in two parts at right angles to each other. Nothing remains of the castle destroyed in the Hundred Years War, but part of the ramparts and three fortified gates are reminders that it was once an important strongpoint.

Accommodation

Outside the village, the **Hôtel Beauregard**, route de Trémolat, 24510 Limeuil (tel: 53 63 30 85), is a modern establishment in the Logis de France organisation in a setting with panoramic views. The restaurant offers cuisine in the best local tradition.

◆◆◆
MONPAZIER ✓

10 miles (16km) southeast of Beaumont, 10 miles (16km) southwest of Belvès
Of the many *bastides* in southwest France, Monpazier is the best preserved and the most attractive. It follows the classical pattern of most *bastides*: a parallelogram, with two pairs of main streets intersecting at right angles, and with narrower streets parallel to them. There is a main square in the centre, used as a market and meeting place, surrounded by arcades on four sides, wide enough for two carts to pass each other, so that peasants could bring their produce right into the market place. There is always a church near the market place. All the houses in these 'new towns' of the Middle Ages were the same size: 26 feet (8m) wide and 65½ feet (20m) deep. They were originally separated by very narrow alleys meant as a fire break, but usually used as rubbish dumps. Over the centuries almost all these alleys disappeared as houses were rebuilt and extended. Some had extra storeys added or roofs altered, so that today the *bastides* do not have the same monotonous uniformity as when they were first built, but have created their own individual characters.
Monpazier was founded in 1289 by Edward I of England, ruler of all Aquitaine at the time. It had a violent and chequered history, changing hands from English to French and back several times during the Hundred Years War,

and from Catholics to Protestants in the Wars of Religion. It was one of the many places that fell to Geoffroy de Vivans, the Protestant soldier. It also had a part in the 17th-century Peasants' Revolt, when a weaver named Buffarot banded together 8,000 peasants and led them in attacks on castles and villages. The revolt lasted three months, from April to June of 1637, and was only put down when Cardinal Richelieu sent in the army. Buffarot was captured and sentenced to death and, on 6 August 1637, he was broken on the wheel in the main square of Monpazier.

It seems incredible that, after all this violence, Monpazier should have survived into the 20th century almost unchanged from what it was 700 years ago, but it has. Today it is a charming village, whose peace is disturbed only by summer tourists, and by the spring and autumn mushroom markets for which it is famous, and which bring buyers from as far afield as Paris. It does have one or two smart shops and restaurants, but remains unspoiled by the passage of time and crowds.

Accommodation

Monpazier has two small hotels of average standard. The **Hôtel de France**, 24540 Monpazier (tel: 53 22 60 06) is a real *auberge* in the old style, in a 13th-century building. Unpretentious, and both rooms and meals are inexpensive. The **Hôtel de Londres**, 24540 Monpazier (tel: 53 22 60 64) offers accommodation at very reasonable cost, and is somewhat less old-fashioned in its style.

Monpazier was built to strict bastide *specifications: eight blocks round a square, with wide arcades to allow carts to pass*

Restaurants

Le Menestrel, 12 place des Cornieres (tel: 53 22 61 14), on the main square, is a clean and cheerful little restaurant, open every day, which offers traditional Périgord cuisine at moderate prices. The **Restaurant de la Bastide**, 52 rue St-Jacques (tel: 53 22 60 59), is much larger and rather more ambitious and expensive, though it has a cheap menu. Dining room with pleasant rustic décor.

MONTIGNAC

15 miles (24km) from Les Eyzies, on D706

Montignac is a pleasant little town on the banks of the Vézère, and was unknown before the discovery of Lascaux (see page 13). Though the original Lascaux was easily the most spectacular of the caves with prehistoric art, there are several others in the area of Montignac and Les Eyzies (see page 67), and some of them have been known much longer. Montignac is useful as a base from which to visit these fascinating caves.

Accommodation

There are two very good hotels in Montignac. The very upmarket **Hôtel Château de Puy Robert** (tel: 53 51 92 13), about a mile (1.5km) outside the town on the D65 going south, is expensive but has comfortable modern rooms (either in the small château itself or in the recently built annexe), a swimming pool in the grounds, and a superb restaurant. Closed from mid-October to April. **Hostellerie le Relais du Soleil d'Or** (tel: 53 51 80 22) is a serious rival, though somewhat cheaper in rooms and restaurants, and is set in an old park with majestic trees and a swimming pool.

A more modest establishment, **Le Lascaux**, 109 avenue Jean Jarès (tel: 53 51 82 81), in Montignac itself, has reasonably priced rooms and a good value restaurant, and is a Logis de France.

ROCAMADOUR ✓

on the D673, 22 miles (35km) southeast of Sarlat-la-Canéda

To the south east of Rocamadour (in the department of Lot), close to the village of L'Hospitalet, there is a viewpoint – beside the appropriately named Hôtel Belvederè. From here the view of Rocamadour, apparently defying gravity as it clings to a vertical cliff, is breathtaking. It is easy to see why a recent survey suggested that this was one of the most-visited villages in France. There was a chapel here from at least the 12th century, but in 1166, grave-diggers unearthed the body of a man. Almost immediately miracles started to occur near the site. By the 15th century the body was accepted as that of Zaccheus, the publican whose wife, St-Veronica, had wiped Christ's face on his journey to Calvary. Rocamadour's fame spread, with as many as 30,000 pilgrims arriving from all over France to attend *pardons* at the church. It is said that when

Protestants captured the village during the Wars of Religion their attempt to destroy the body was foiled when it refused to burn. Today's visitor can follow in the footsteps of the medieval pilgrims climbing up through the village to the ramparts high above, a marvellous viewpoint. At the nearby Rocher des Aigles (Eagles' Rock) there is a breeding centre for birds of prey, with regular displays of falconry.

♦♦♦
LA ROQUE-GAGEAC ✓

1 mile (2km) east of Beynac on the north bank of the Dordogne, on the D703
You could spend a fortnight in this part of the Dordogne valley and visit a different picturesque village and its spectacular castle each day. La Roque-Gageac has, in the past, been awarded the title of the prettiest village in France. From a distance, its golden stone houses seem to be piled one on top of the other as they climb the face of their protective cliff. It is a very well-known beauty spot now, and on Sundays in summer, getting through it along the narrow road by the river can be something of a scramble. It is a pleasant village to walk around: some of the higher streets have enchanting views of the river between the houses.
At the western end, the apparently 15th-century **Château de la Malartrie** is really an early 20th-century imitation of the earlier style. At the other side of the village there is a fine period house with

Famous for its links with the Lascaux caves, Montignac is an attractive town on the Vézère

a round tower – the manor of the Tarde family. Jean Tarde was Vicar General of the diocese of Sarlat at the end of the 16th century.

Accommodation
Hôtel La Belle Etoile, 24250 La Roque-Gageac (tel: 53 29 51 44). Very pleasant little hotel just across the road from the river.

♦
ST-AMAND-DE-COLY
4 miles (6km) east of Montignac
The ancient village of St-Amand-de-Coly, a haunt of artists and craftsmen, nestles in a side valley of the Vézère. Its old houses are dominated by one of the best examples of a fortified

PÉRIGORD NOIR

The village of La Roque-Gageac

medieval church to be found anywhere in France. It seems far too big and important for so small a village, but the church was once the centre of a big Augustinian monastery, and is now all that remains of it.
The bare, almost windowless walls give the building a certain grandeur. The most obvious of the defensive features are on the west front, both porch and keep. The height and simplicity of the interior are impressive, and there are some defensive elements, even within the church, hidden stairways, and some hollow pillars.

◆◆
ST-LÉON-SUR-VÉZÈRE
off the D706, between Montignac and Les Eyzies
St-Léon-sur-Vézère is a charming village, set in a lovely

bend of the river. It has a fine example of a 12th-century Romanesque church, with roofs of the attractive stone tiles called *lauzes*. Inside there is a 16th-century seated Virgin and child. Concerts of classical music are given in the church during July and August.

◆◆◆
SARLAT-LA-CANÉDA ✓
13 miles (21km) from Les Eyzies on the D47; 15¼ miles (25km) from Montignac on the D704
The capital of Périgord Noir, and a *sous-préfecture* of the Dordogne department, Sarlat has more medieval, Renaissance and 18th-century façades, carved doorways, fountains, turrets, gables and unusual roofscapes than could be photographed in a week of fine days, but driving through allows you to see none of all this.

The main road through the town, the rue de la République, called in Sarlat 'the Traverse', is a purely commercial street, from which none of the old town can be seen. Sarlat has to be explored on foot, and it needs at least a morning or an afternoon to see the best of it.

Like many other small towns in France, Sarlat owes its origin to the monks. It grew up around a Benedictine Abbey, founded well over a thousand years ago. It became a bishopric in the 14th century, and remained one until the French Revolution. During the Hundred Years War, it lay between English and French controlled territories, and was often attacked by one side or the other, until it was assigned to the English by the terms of the Treaty of Bretigny in 1360. It became French again before the end of the war. A Catholic town, it was several times attacked during the religious wars of the 16th century, but the people were stubborn defenders, and only that audacious and resourceful Protestant captain, Geoffroy de Vivans, succeeded in capturing and sacking the town. In February 1574, he led his soldiers in disguise into the town while the inhabitants were holding a carnival and completely unprepared for fighting. In 1587 another Protestant leader, the Vicomte de Turenne, besieged the town, but it held out.

Since then, it has been left in peace, but it is only recently that it has found any prosperity. Most early guide books, and all those published more than 30 years ago, ignore Sarlat altogether, or mention it only to say how old, dirty and tumble-down it was. Many ancient buildings had survived, but they were invariably in a dilapidated and maltreated condition. The town had always considered itself too poor to do anything about them, and as the rue de la République was driven straight through the middle of the old part in 1837, knocking down everything in the way, and with no attempt at preservation, they clearly had no regard for them anyway.

Today Sarlat attracts more than half a million visitors every year, most of them during July and August. The change is due to one remarkable man, André Malraux, who was de Gaulle's Minister for Propaganda and later Minister for Cultural Affairs. In 1962 he introduced *la loi Malraux*, to provide for the restoration of old buildings and sectors of certain towns. Since then, more than 70 old buildings in Sarlat have been restored.

Beyond the south doorway of St-**Sacerdos Cathedral** there is a courtyard closed on the south side by the **Chapel of the Blue Penitents**, a Romanesque building in sober style. In the 14th century, societies of voluntary penitents were formed. They took it upon themselves to absolve the sins of others, which they did by performing unpleasant tasks, such as caring for lepers. In another part of the town there is a **Chapel of White Penitents**, which now houses a museum of sacred objects and souvenirs of old Sarlat, and is open morning and afternoon, Easter to November, except Sunday mornings.

PÉRIGORD NOIR

If you walk through the **Cour des Fontaines**, (Fountain Courtyard) behind the Chapel of the Blue Penitents, you will find stone steps leading up the hill to a curious tower known as the **Lanterne des Morts**, or Lantern of the Dead. It has been suggested that the bodies of the dead in epidemics were placed there, but it is not really known what it was used for. The **place de la Liberté**, in the centre of the town, is surrounded by Renaissance mansions and medieval houses. Just behind the Tourist Office is the **Hôtel Maleville** (*hôtel* originally meant a large town house), which was created in the 16th century, when three houses were converted into a mansion with corbelled towers.

Pedestrians see the best of the old town of Sarlat and its architectural variety

On Saturday mornings the place de la Liberté is the scene of one of the most famous and lively markets in Périgord. Sarlat has long been well known for its geese and ducks, and the *confit* and *foie gras* made from them, and if you walk up through the place de la Liberté you find, just beyond the partly demolished and disaffected Church of St-Mary, the **place des Oies** (Goose Market).

There are several fine houses in the nearby rue des Consuls, of which the most striking is the **Hôtel Plamon**. It was built in the 14th century by the Selvès de Plamon family, who made their money as cloth merchants. There are other fine houses in the angle of the street by the place des Oies, known as **Les Maisons des Consuls** and, on the other side of the street, the 15th-century **Hôtel Vassal**, with double turrets, and the **Hôtel Gisson**.

Beside the cathedral, in the place du Peyrou, there is a café terrace, which is a popular place from which to watch the world go by.

Just across the square from the café is the façade of the **Maison de la Boétie**, one of the finest Renaissance houses in Sarlat. It was built in the early 16th century by Antoine de la Boétie, the father of Étienne, friend of the essayist Michel de Montaigne. The writings of Étienne de la Boétie are said to have inspired Jean-Jacques Rousseau when he came to write the Social Contract, which contributed to the background of the French Revolution. The Maison de la Boétie is a lavishly furnished house, with decorative gables and carved stonework around the windows. When La Boétie died there in 1553, Montaigne (see page 46) was at his bedside.

Sarlat is a captivating town, even though, in the high season, it sometimes resembles a festival or a fairground, rather more than the historical monument which it is. It is a shame, also, that there are not more interiors to be seen. There are so many façades that it sometimes feels like an elaborate Hollywood film set, an impression heightened because the ready-made audience attracts attention-seekers who look as if they are taking a few minutes off from some bizarre film.

Every year Sarlat has a musical and theatrical festival (Le Festival des Jeux du Théâtre) from 15 July to 15 August. It attracts some fine performers, and is set in the **place de la Liberté**, against the background of the Église Ste-Marie and adjacent Renaissance houses. The rue de la République (*La Traverse*) is one of the most intensely commercial streets in Périgord, and is a good hunting ground for souvenirs, particularly the gastronomic products of the region.

Accommodation

There is a heavy demand for accommodation in Sarlat in summer, and it is important to reserve in advance.
Hostellerie Marcel, 8 avenue de Selvès (tel: 53 59 21 98). An unpretentious and modestly priced hotel, welcoming, and with a restaurant which offers excellent value.

Hôtel de la Madeleine, 1 place de la Petite Rigaudie (tel: 53 59 10 41). This is a long-established hotel and still a favourite, with a restaurant well known for the quality of its traditional Périgord cuisine. A comfortable, well-managed hotel. Prices for both meals and rooms a little above average.

Hôtel St-Albert, 10 place Pasteur (tel: 53 31 55 55). With the recently added Hotel Montaigne, forms the largest hotel complex in Sarlat. Reliable, though it seems at times rather a 'tourist factory'. The restaurant, in the St-Albert, is popular, and moderately priced.

Outside the Town

Hôtel La Hoirie, à la Canéda, 24200 Sarlat (tel: 53 59 05 62). Just over a mile (2km) south of Sarlat by the Gourdon road (D704 and then C1), this is an old Périgord house, a former hunting lodge of the same Vienne family who owned the Hôtel de Maleville in town. Pleasantly set in a wooded park with a swimming pool. Comfortable rooms, good bathrooms, and a restaurant. Nice, but rather expensive.

Hostellerie de Meysset, Lieu dit Argentouleau, 24200 Sarlat (tel: 53 59 08 29), at Argentouleau, just over a mile (2km) out of town by the Les Eyzies road (D6). A nice country house in a wooded park on top of a hill; good views. Pleasant terrace for outdoor meals, small but comfortable rooms, and a restaurant well above average. Good, but you pay a full price for what you get.

◆

TRÉMOLAT

on the D31 west of Limeuil

The picturesque route to Trémolat from Limeuil (see page 74) has several viewpoints over the famous *Cingle* de Trémolat. *Cingle* means 'loop', and at this point the Dordogne, diverted by harder rocks, sweeps round in a great loop. The best views are from the **Panoramic Hotel**, and from the **Belvedere de Rocamadour**, reached by a rough and poorly signposted side road. From either point you look down upon an idyllic scene of neatly tilled fields between the great arms of the river, crossed by golden stone bridges, its banks lined with tall poplars.

The level of water in this part of the Dordogne has been controlled and raised by the barrage at **Mauzac**, a few miles downstream, enabling Trémolat to become a centre for all kinds of summerwater sports.

It is a good idea to cross the river at Trémolat (if you have continued to the viewpoint at Rocamadour, you will have to return a couple of miles) and to continue by way of Traly to Cales, and then by the D29 to **Badefols-sur-Dordogne**, where there is a ruined castle, once the base of the river pirates who exacted severe tolls from all the river traffic.

Recross the river at **Lalinde**, founded by the English in 1267 as a *bastide* but much knocked about over the centuries and hardly recognisable as such today. It is now a prosperous commercial centre and market, with some industrialisation. It is of little interest to the tourist, except that it does have cafés, restaurants, and several hotels. From Lalinde the D29 continues to **Couze-et-St-Front**, where the fast-flowing Couze enters the Dordogne. Couze was the centre of an important paper-making industry for hundreds of years, the first mills having been founded in the 15th century. They produced high quality papers but there are not so many working mills today. Some still in operation specialise in filter and blotting papers, and one is still producing hand-made papers.

Accommodation

The **Hôtel le Panoramic**, route du Cingle (tel: 53 22 80 42), is a well run, comfortable hotel, with moderately priced rooms and a sound restaurant. It is about a mile (2km) from Trémolat. The other local hotel, **Le Vieux Logis**, Trémolat (tel: 53 22 80 06), is in the village itself, though surrounded by its own immaculate lawns and flower gardens. It is an exceptional hotel, reaching standards of furnishing and comfort rarely found in the provinces, yet still completely in tune with its country surroundings. The excellent restaurant, specialising in traditional Périgord cuisine, is rather expensive, and the bedrooms more so.

In Lalinde, the **Hôtel du Château**, 1 rue Verdun (tel: 53 61 01 82), is housed in a building which was once the small fortress of the *bastide*. It is a Logis de France, reasonably priced.

The **Hôtel La Forge**, place Victor Hugo (tel: 53 24 92 24) is also a Logis de France but is larger, and has a cheaper restaurant, but more expensive bedrooms.

Trémolat, where the Dordogne forms a perfect horseshoe bend

THE RIVER VALLEY

The Dordogne river itself warrants exploration. There are many beauty spots and places of historical interest worth visiting eastwards along the river valley, and, although they lie beyond the Dordogne department, they are within easy reach of bases inside Dordogne.

WHAT TO SEE

◆◆
CARENNAC
on the D43, south of the River Dordogne, about 15 miles (24km) east of Souillac, via Martel and Floirac

A jumble of red roofs clusters round the old abbey where the writer-priest François de Salignac de la Mothe Fénelon was prior in the late 17th century. Here, where the Dordogne sweeps round small islands, he wrote his story of the son of Ulysses, Telemachus (*Télémaque*). His eloquence in defence of persuasion rather than violence in converting the Protestants, and his literary fame, gained him a reputation in the Church, and he was made Archbishop of Cambrai, in the far north. The priory was heavily damaged at the time of the Revolution, but the village itself still has 16th-century houses, and has changed little since Fénelon's day. The porch of the Romanesque Church of St-Pierre has a lovely 12th-century carved doorway, and there are cloisters (restored) with three Flamboyant Gothic sides and one Romanesque.

◆
CREYSSE
on the D23 south of Martel, which is 9 miles (14km) east of Souillac by the D703

Creysse is an old-world village in a loop of the river, with a little square shaded by plane trees, ancient houses with flights of stone steps outside and vines and flowers, with an old church and the ruins of a castle looking down on the rusty brown roofs. From Creysse, the route north and east through the Dordogne valley approaches the Massif Central, and the roads become a little difficult, but are so picturesque that it is worth a little map-reading effort to make your way to **Gluges**, and then back across to the south side of the river to the **Cirque de Montvalent**, and then to **Floirac** and **Cerennac**.

*A view of the Dordogne, from the
fortress of Castelnaud (see pages
60–1)*

◆◆◆
GOUFFRE DE PADIRAC ✓

*6 miles (10km) south of
Carennac via D20 and D60*
The Devil, returning to Hell with
a sackful of souls, met St Martin
riding a donkey along a track on
the plateau south of the
Dordogne Valley. Being a
gambling man, the Devil offered
the saint the chance to win back
the souls if he could make his
donkey cross an obstacle of the
Devil's choosing. If he failed, the
saint's soul would be added to
the sack. St Martin agreed and
the Devil thumped the floor with
his foot, creating a vast hole.
Undaunted by its size and
depth, St Martin urged his

donkey forward, and the animal
jumped across the hole.
St Martin won the sack and the
Devil retreated back to Hell
down the hole he had created.
This legend illustrates the awe in
which the locals held the Padirac
cave until Edouard Martel, the
father of the science of
speleology, explored it in the
late 19th century. Today's
explorer is assisted by lifts and a
boat 550 yards (500m) along an
underground river to the
sparkling Lac de la Pluie (Lake of
Rain) as he follows in Martel's
footsteps through a magical
world of beautiful stalagmites,
stalactites and rock formations.
One stalactite, the Grande
Pendeloque (Great Pendant), is
256 feet (78m) long and almost
touches the water the visitor's
boat crosses.
Open: daily, April to mid-October.

THE RIVER VALLEY

Gabariers

The Dordogne has been a major trade route since earliest times, but its variable flow made it a dangerous as well as a useful highway. The perils of seasonal floodwaters were met by a hardy breed of boatmen called *gabariers* who used flat-bottomed boats to brave the river. These boats were usually called *gabardes*, but were also known as *sapines*, or *argentats*, after the town of Argentat on the Upper Dordogne. The *gabariers* took leather, wine and cheese downriver to the Garonne and Bordeaux, the trip sometimes taking many weeks.

Visitors to the Dordogne who wish to see a *gabarde* should go to Argentat, north east of Sarlat-la-Canéda and, though on the river, just outside the area covered by this book. There, the original river quay has been preserved and *gabardes* are tied up just as they were years ago.

◆
MARTEL

on the D703, 9 miles (15km) east of Souillac

In AD 732 the French leader, Charles Martel, halted the Moorish invasion near Poitiers, and a few years later he defeated them completely near the Dordogne. To offer thanks he had a church built on the spot. A town grew up around it and was named Martel, in his honour. Now a quiet little agricultural centre, known for its market in truffles and nuts, Martel still has many medieval buildings.

SOUILLAC

18 miles (29km) east of Sarlat, on D703 junction with N20

Souillac is a pleasant little town with one of the finest religious buildings in this area: the domed 12th-century church which is all that remains of its Benedictine monastery. The abbey was dissolved at the time of the Revolution, and the building is now the parish church of Ste-Marie. The interior is sober in style, but at the end of the nave there is a beautifully carved doorway, brought inside when the church was restored. The tympanum tells the story of a monk, Theophilus, who made a bargain with the Devil but repented and prayed to the Virgin for his soul to be saved. The right hand pillar has some carvings of monstrous animals. There are also fine carvings of the prophets Isaiah and Joseph, mounting guard on either side of the door.

Accommodation

La Vieille Auberge, 1 place de la Minoterie (tel: 65 32 79 43), is a pleasant inn; Logis de France. **Les Granges Vieilles**, route de Sarlat (tel: 65 37 80 92), is a comfortable Logis de France.

Restaurants

Souillac has a good choice of restaurants, of which the **Auberge du Puits** (tel: 65 37 80 32), in the heart of the old town, deserves a special mention. This long-established inn has a restaurant that offers the best traditional cuisine at unbeatable prices, and economical rooms.

PEACE AND QUIET

Wildlife and Countryside in Dordogne
by Paul Sterry

Dordogne is one of the most beautiful regions in lowland France. Rivers such as the Dordogne, the Vézère and the nearby Garonne wind through lush, lowland valleys, often overlooked by charming French towns. Hills rise away up from the valleys to form plateaux which are often cloaked in forests comprising oak and sweet chestnut. These yield two of the region's most important natural products: chestnuts and truffles. Man and his ancestors have inhabited the area for tens of thousands of years, and the subjects of many of the cave paintings include animals extinct in this part of Europe since the last Ice Age. Men have made

Truffles are the richest prize to be found in Dordogne woodlands

their mark, not only in the walls of the limestone caves for which the region is famous, but also on the landscape of the Dordogne area as a whole. Although hydro-electric schemes have changed the appearance of the upland reaches of the River Dordogne, and many of the forests have been felled, making way for moorland and agricultural land, the scenery and wildlife of the region cannot fail to enthral.

Agricultural Land
Farming in Dordogne is anything but uniform, and the surprising range of produce grown reflects the varying nature of the underlying soils. Limestone, sandstone, granite and alluvial soils each favour different crops or stock animals, and the aspect of the land also has a strong influence: fields may be sheltered in a river valley, baked on a sunny, south-facing slope or exposed on a wind-swept plateau-top.

PEACE AND QUIET

In many low-lying regions of Dordogne, fruit and vegetables are the main crops. Some of the produce is destined to reach markets elsewhere in Europe early in the year, taking advantage of the region's mild winters and generous rainfall. However, orchards of fruit trees are also a prominent feature, producing apples, cherries, walnuts and plums. Some of the plum varieties, including greengage types, are consumed fresh, while others are dried to make prunes. Dordogne is also the largest strawberry-producing region in the whole of France.

Fruit orchards, especially those not maintained intensively, can be good for wildlife. Black-veined white butterflies flit between the trees, while melodious warblers and even golden orioles feed and occasionally nest inconspicuously in their branches.

Red-backed shrikes feed their young on lizards and insects

Tobacco is another important product of the region, some being used for snuff. Cereals and fodder and oil-producing crops are also commonly grown

Shrikes
Red-backed shrikes frequently perch out in the open, constantly on the look-out for prey. Mantids, bush-crickets and even small lizards fall victim to these sharp-eyed predators, who sometimes have the rather grizzly habit of impaling their prey on thorns or barbed wire. Although this may seem rather gratuitous, it in fact secures the victim so that the shrike can tear pieces off to eat. Unsurprisingly, red-backed shrikes have earned the nickname of 'butcher birds' as a result of this habit.

with maize and sunflowers increasingly favoured. When the plants have reached a height of several feet, the ground beneath often becomes carpeted in bindweed. This serves as a foodplant for the caterpillars of the convolvulus hawk moth, one of the largest insects in Europe, which, despite its size, is camouflaged and difficult to see. During heavy rainstorms, however, they often ascend the crop plants and shelter under the leaves, making them much more easy to spot.

Towns and Smallholdings

Most of the towns and villages in Dordogne are picturesque and lie in settings of classic French scenery. Their proximity to the countryside, combined with the relaxed attitude of most residents, means that gardens in towns and around small farms hold considerable wildlife interest to anyone with a keen eye and ear.

Fruit-bearing trees are commonly grown in gardens and have a wealth of insect life. The songs of cicadas can be almost deafening during the summer months, with many of them falling victim to predatory mantids. Rose-chafer beetles and black-veined white, Camberwell beauty and swallowtail butterflies visit garden flowers for nectar, while bush-crickets like the well-known 'tizi' or saddle-back bush-cricket chirp from low bushes. Day-flying butterflies are often accompanied by hummingbird hawk moths, the skill and manoeuvrability of which as they feed on the wing

is truly amazing. After dark, a different set of insects is attracted to the flowers, including large species such as bedstraw and striped hawk moths. They in turn attract numerous bats, which are often seen flying around outside lamps catching the unfortunate insects which they lure. Gardens, and particularly those which are overgrown, are a haven for birds. Warblers such as blackcap and lesser whitethroat scold from the cover of vegetation, while swallows twitter around the eaves of buildings and outhouses. Large lawns may even attract the exotic-looking hoopoe, a pink bird with chequered wings and a long, curved beak.

Although grown on a large scale on plantations in the region, walnut trees grace the gardens of almost every small farm. They are of great commercial importance to the region as a whole, Dordogne being France's greatest producer, but they are also used in everyday local cooking, most noticeably in walnut bread.

What makes the trees of special interest for those interested in wildlife is the serins which nest in them. The males are among Dordogne's most attractive garden residents, making up for their tiny size with bright yellow plumage and an attractive, jingling song, which sounds similar to their close relative, the canary.

Woodlands of Dordogne

With the abundance of potential firewood in Dordogne, it is not surprising that the region's

PEACE AND QUIET

dense forests gradually dwindled. The average lifespan of the trees also became shorter, because the biggest trees were felled, with the result that today's woodlands contain relatively small specimens.

Man's Impact in Dordogne
Prehistoric cave paintings and flint arrowheads bear witness to the fact that Dordogne has been inhabited by mankind and his ancestors for more than 100,000 years. During this time he has had a profound effect on the scenery of the region, this being most strikingly demonstrated by the clearance of forests which at one time cloaked the land.
Flint axes would originally have been used to fell the trees, the timber being used for tools and buildings, and there is evidence that as far back as 150,000 years ago, men had the ability to create fire with flints.

Nowadays, more modern methods are used to fell the trees, some of the timber becoming charcoal for the glass industry, while oak is used to make wine barrels.
The woodlands that survive often differ markedly in character from one another. On the more acidic granite plateaux soils, oaks are common, while elsewhere, where the underlying rock is limestone, mixed woodlands occur. Lower slopes harbour sweet chestnuts, the seeds of which are roasted or puréed, and plantation woodlands of this crop are also grown.
The cool, damp winters that favour the fungi of the region also encourage slugs and snails, particularly on limestone soils (the calcium is essential in shell production). The largest species in the region is the edible or Roman snail which is such a popular part of French cuisine.

Woodland and Wildlife
The woodlands of the Dordogne region offer anyone with an interest in wildlife hours of fascination. Mosses and liverworts grow on tree stumps and branches, while birds sing from the canopy above. Although requiring patience to see them, a range of woodland mammals may reward the persistent observer.
Four species of woodpecker are regularly seen in Dordogne's woodlands, and their undulating flight from tree to tree is a familiar sight. Green wood-peckers are easily recognised by their green and yellow plumage and loud yelping call. Lesser spotted, the smallest woodpeckers in Europe, are barely bigger than a sparrow. The other two species, great-spotted and middle-spotted woodpecker, are potentially confusing and the patterns of black and red on the head should be studied closely.
Great, marsh and crested tits nest in the older woodlands and outside the breeding season roam far and wide, often in flocks of mixed species.
By contrast with the birds, woodland mammals are harder to see. Pine and beech martens and the cat-like genet are secretive and largely nocturnal, shunning human presence. Wild boar still roam the woods and,

Woodland Songsters

In spring, the flute-like song of the golden oriole is a characteristic sound. Many pass through the region on migration to northern Europe but some stay to breed, building curious suspended nests high in the tree canopy. Nightingales and blackcaps are also common and add to the richness of bird-song. Although not as far-carrying as the nightingale's song, that of the blackcap is a lovely warble, which has a similar quality to a blackbird's song.

In Roman times, edible dormice were considered a delicacy. Luckily for them, tastes change

despite human persecution, will sometimes even raid rubbish bins in more secluded spots. One of the most interesting mammals of the region is the edible dormouse, a squirrel-like species with a long bushy tail, which was considered a delicacy in Roman times. Although largely nocturnal, these agile climbers are sometimes active during the day in the summer when small family parties can be seen leaping from branch to branch.

Plateaux

Much of this region of France is dominated by plateaux of rolling hills, off which the many rivers of the region run. They range from 1,600 feet (500m) above sea level to 3,200 feet (1,000m) in Limousin and although comparatively low by the standards of hills and mountains elsewhere in France, the plateaux possess great variety as a result of the nature of the underlying rock. This ranges from granite to limestone and affects both the scenery and the vegetation, producing thickly wooded slopes, open moorland, green pastures and dramatic gorges.

At one time oak and mixed wood-land covered the plateaux and

PEACE AND QUIET

The aptly named map butterfly has fine markings on the underwing

although there are still extensive forests left, much of the land has been cleared of trees. On those hills which have not come under the plough and where the underlying rock is granite, heath and moorland communities of plants and animals have developed. The pinks and purples of heathers and the yellow flowers of gorse and broom are attractive throughout the summer and harbour nesting Dartford warblers, whitethroats and stonechats. Occasionally, a hobby may be seen gliding effortlessly over the moorland in search of dragonflies or small birds which it catches with ease in flight. Granite is one of the most ancient of all rocks and is a source of uranium, which is mined in the region.
Limestone plateaux, such as those in Quercy and Périgord, generally have a greener appearance, especially where a short grassy turf has been produced by the grazing of generations of sheep. These pastures are often rich in flower species, and in particular

orchids. Burnt, bee and early spider orchids grow in the open, while in clearings in open, scrubby woodland, the lucky visitor may find colonies of sword-leaved helleborine and fly, military and man orchids. Rainfall is always slightly acid due to the presence of dissolved carbonic acid. While this does little to erode resistant rocks like granite, where the water runs over limestone it dissolves it, in the end producing Dordogne's famous gorges and caves.

Butterflies
Butterflies are a beautiful and conspicuous feature of Dordogne's wildlife and range in size from the diminutive little blue to the impressive swallow-tail. Dozens of species occur in the region. Since each one flies at a different time of year, butterflies of one sort or another can be seen from March right through until September. It is always surprising to see butterflies on the wing as early as March when even the daytime temperatures can be cool. While some species, such as the Bath white, will have emerged from overwintering pupae, others will have hibernated as adults. Elegant white-bordered Camberwell beauties and large tortoiseshells are both woodland species who spend the winters in holes in trees or in caves. They emerge to catch the first warmth of spring along with brimstone butterflies, which roost among leaves.
As the year progresses, the open woodlands of Dordogne see the first generations of black-veined whites, wood whites and map

butterflies. The undersides of the latter species are finely netted and veined, giving the impression of a medieval map. Later in the summer, ilex, purple, brown and black hairstreaks appear, the first two being associated with oak and the latter with blackthorn. All these butterflies are extremely active in the heat of the summer but can sometimes be approached closely with a camera, while they feed on the nectar from flowers and honeydew on leaves. Meadows in lowland valleys are the haunt of colourful swallowtail butterflies, while on hillsides, especially where vetches and clovers grow in abundance, clouded yellows, pale clouded yellows, long-tailed and mazarine blues and fritillaries are common. During the middle of the day, they are all active and wary of danger, but if you want to photograph them try visiting the same meadow at dawn.

Hunters and the Hunted

Animals have always been hunted in Dordogne, as the cave paintings of bison, mammoths and reindeer testify. In the past, however, the quarry was generally hunted for food, but nowadays, animals are also shot and trapped for 'sport' and an unnecessary fate befalls many birds of prey in the region. However, despite persecution, the wooded slopes of Dordogne, which once harboured wolves and bears, are still the haunt of a variety of fascinating raptors. Sparrowhawks are often seen floating over their nesting territory in display. Buzzards and honey buzzards are also common and potentially confusing in appearance. The year-round resident buzzards always have dark carpal patches on their wings, and a loud, cat-like

Snakes are a major part of the diet of the short-toed eagle

mewing call which is distinctive and far-carrying.

Honey buzzards, on the other hand, are usually silent and the most distinctive feature in flight is their strongly barred wings and the dark band near the end of the tail. Whereas buzzards feed mostly on carrion and earthworms, honey buzzards, as their name implies, raid the nests of wild bees and wasps, feeding, however, not on the honey but on the grubs.

Lizards bask in the open on stony ground. Many fall victim to snakes such as the asp, adder and Aesculapian snake which specialise in preying upon their reptilian cousins. Asps are rather shy snakes, preferring to retreat to cover if disturbed; Aesculapian snakes are bolder and will sometimes stand their ground if cornered. When confronted with a snake that can

Dordogne Dovecotes

In medieval times it was common for many families and villages in Dordogne to have their own dovecotes. Strangely the dovecotes were usually erected not for the collection of eggs or fat young birds for the kitchen, but for the *guano* the birds produced. Pigeon droppings are an excellent fertiliser and, remarkably were also used by local bakers who claimed that a sprinkling added an extra piquancy to their bread!

Dovecotes took a variety of forms, the most common being the *suspendu* in which the pigeonhouse was held aloft on columns which protected the birds from damp and predators.

grow to as much as 80 inches (200cm) in length, it is difficult not to feel intimidated.

La Brenne

Although La Brenne is about a two-hour drive north of Dordogne, its terrain offers a striking contrast to that area's woodlands, plateaux and agricultural land, and makes a visit particularly worthwhile for the birdwatcher. The region is easily reached by taking the N21 north from Périgueux to Limoges, and then the N20 towards Châteauroux.

Hundreds of lakes and ponds, many of which are easily viewed from the roads, make up a wetland patchwork to the north of the River Creuze west of Châteauroux and are a haven for water-loving birds and a well-known route for migrant species. Although there is a certain amount of hunting here, it is more prevalent in autumn and winter and so breeding birds can, in the main, nest in peace. Many of the larger lakes have extensive reed-beds around their margins, which provide a sanctuary for most of the nesting species. All three European species of harrier breed here, with marsh and Montagu's being particularly common. They can frequently be seen quartering the reedbeds and surrounding agricultural fields in search of small mammals and birds, or perched on fence posts which provide ideal lookouts.

Savi's, reed and great reed warblers nest in the reedbeds and their songs fill the air in spring. The loud booming call of the bittern is a far-carrying and familiar sound, while the croaking call of the little bittern might easily be confused with one of the many frogs and toads found here. Elegant and shy purple herons are also numerous, sometimes building their platform nests of dead reeds in small communal groups. At dusk, Baillon's crakes and water rails sometimes venture out of cover to feed on the muddy margins of the ponds and lakes, while the open water is favoured by great-crested, black-necked and little grebes which dive for fish. Insects and small fish at the water's surface attract whiskered and black terns, which nest in La Brenne, and wheeling flocks of both species are frequently seen. The surrounding farmland is good for birds of prey, with harriers and kestrels being most common.

Purple herons nest in dense reedbeds. Their diet comprises mainly frogs and fish

Ground-dwelling birds can be difficult to see during spring and summer because they remain hidden by the crops but in early spring, when the vegetation is short and after the harvest in autumn, the keen-eyed observer may find little bustards and stone curlews.

The River Dordogne
The River Dordogne is one of the longest in France. From its origins at the confluence of the Dore and the Dogne in the Massif Central, it cascades through steep gorges, then winds gently through fertile valleys. Eventually, it joins the Garonne and as the Gironde forms a huge estuary and floodplain as it enters the sea beyond Bordeaux. Although great dams and hydro-electric schemes have dramatically altered the river's appearance in its upper reaches, downstream of these the Dordogne has not changed for centuries.

PEACE AND QUIET

In parts of eastern Dordogne unaffected by hydro-electric schemes, the river is too turbulent for delicate aquatic animals to survive. Caddis fly larvae protect themselves by building little cases of sand and gravel, while stonefly larvae glue their cases to boulders to prevent them being swept away.

Despite the rigours of the - environment, a few birds still manage to find enough to eat. Dippers are often seen flying low over the water, or perched on exposed rocks in the river. They flick their tails and bob up and down, but their name is derived from their habit of walking and swimming under the water in order to collect the insect larvae and small fish.

Grey wagtails also nest along the riverbanks and under bridges, their shrill call and wagging tail making them easy to recognise. Their diet consists almost exclusively of adult insects which have emerged from aquatic larvae in the river. The upper reaches of the Dordogne harbour a variety of fish including gudgeon, bullheads and even trout. Although the dams have interrupted the migration of trout from lower reaches of the river, populations still survive above the reservoirs.

The Freshwater Environment

Despite its rugged, upland plateaux, the Dordogne region is dissected by rivers and valleys and boasts an interesting variety of lowland freshwater habitats. Ponds and lakes, some of which are man-made, attract both resident and tourist fishermen alike and offer plenty of interest

to the wildlife enthusiast. Vineyards, orchards, cereals and tobacco all grow well in these valleys and in some areas, traditional meadows are grazed by cattle. Where these have not been 'improved' with fertilisers and seeded grasses, they are full of colourful wild flowers in spring and summer which attract insects to feed on the nectar. Fennel is a common umbellifer which can be found in wet ditches as well as meadows, and its feathery leaves, which smell of aniseed, are eaten by the poisonous caterpillars of swallowtail butterflies.

The waters of the Dordogne and its fellow rivers harbour a rich variety of fish, many of which are keenly sought by anglers and feature on the menus of local restaurants. Grayling, barbel and trout prefer the faster flowing currents, while backwaters are favoured by bream, roach and bleak and the larger, predatory pike and perch.

There are numerous ponds and lakes throughout the region, many of which are used for swimming but are also stocked with fish. Predatory dragonflies and damselflies patrol the water's surface in search of smaller insects while underwater, perch and carp rise to catch creatures trapped at the surface.

The Dordogne's abundant fish-life also encourages fish-eating birds. Grey herons stalk pond and river margins while kingfishers perch on overhanging branches waiting for smaller prey to swim into range before diving into the water. They fly fast and low over the water and often a flash of iridescent blue is all that is seen.

FOOD AND DRINK

Périgord is well known throughout France for the excellence of its cuisine. It is a richness based on the superb quality of the natural products of the region.

There are deer and wild boar in the forests, partridge, pheasant, quail and hare in the fields and woods. The rivers and lakes abound with trout, crayfish, pike, sander and other good fish. There is hardly a farm without its geese, ducks, pigs and chickens, all of excellent quality. As well as game in the woods there is the famous truffle, and about a dozen other kinds of edible mushrooms, including the delicious *cèpe de Bordeaux*. The valleys are full of walnut trees, as well as chestnuts and hazelnuts. There are delicious locally grown fruits and berries of all kinds to fill the market stalls, and which are used in the making of liqueurs of all sorts. Dordogne is the largest producer of strawberries in France.

Restaurants

Eating out is still one of the great bargains in France. Prices vary from about 80 francs per head for a straightforward three-course meal, sometimes with house wine included, in an ordinary country restaurant, to 500 francs per head for a gourmet meal in the very best restaurants.

Whatever your choice it is very rare not to get value for money. The timid eater who fears to venture beyond roast chicken, or steak and salad, or fish and chips, will miss the wonders offered by the cooks of

Walnut mousse – made from some of Périgord's local produce

FOOD AND DRINK

Périgord. It is true that there are some cynical restaurateurs who, discouraged and conditioned by unadventurous clients, just give tourists what they ask for. But there are still many places where the discriminating visitor can find gourmet meals at reasonable prices.

Most meals in Périgord begin with a soup, usually thick. The Périgordins believe that it aids digestion and enables wine to be taken without ill effect. Restaurants offering traditional meals at bargain prices are harder to find in touristic areas of the Périgord Noir, though even here it is still possible to get very good value.

Where there is a choice of restaurants, remember that by law in France menus and prices must be shown *outside*. Compare them. In general, prefer restaurants with short menus to those that seem to list dozens of possibilities. Some places have the dubious habit of posting up prices in large figures near the 'Restaurant' sign, but when you look at the actual menu you find, particularly on the cheapest menu, that there is hardly a dish without an eight or 10 franc supplement. So watch out.

If you eat *à la carte*, you need only take one dish, and this is often the cheapest thing to do, when you are not hungry. There is no reason why a diner who is entitled to something on his menu which he doesn't want – it might be soup, cheese or dessert – should not give it to another person who has ordered only one dish, *à la carte*.

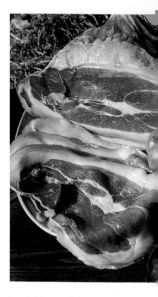

In addition to *à la carte*, most restaurants offer a choice of about three separate *menus*, that is fixed-price set meals. The price difference between one menu and the other reflects differences not only in quality, but in quantity (*ie* number of courses). A menu meal generally offers the best value providing you find one to match your tastes.

Specialities

Foremost of these is that rare and mysterious fungus, the black truffle. As it is impossible to cultivate commercially and has to be searched out in the wild, it becomes more and more expensive as the demand for it increases. Though still obtainable in the best restaurants, a helping of genuine truffle tart now costs at

Ham: a Dordogne speciality, but served in a variety of ways, according to individual taste

but it was realised that specially trained dogs, usually bitches, were less likely to sample them themselves. At about 70 francs a mouthful it was an important point.

The truffle is used in at least 20 characteristic Périgord recipes and it adds a very distinctive flavour, unlike anything else. It is commonly used in omelettes, *foie gras*, and *pâtés*. The trouble is that, because they are so expensive, chefs tend to be sparing in their use and, although you will have little difficulty in finding menus with items with the word *truffé* after them, you may have to search hard to find the few black specks indicating their use, when the dish actually reaches your table.

Foie Gras

Another speciality for which Périgord is famous is *foie gras*, literally 'fat liver'. This is a complicated subject, unfamiliar to many visitors, and one where it is very easy to be misled. *Foie gras* is the official term for goose or duck liver which has been produced by the method known as *gavage*. The selected birds (not all of them are judged suitable) are fed extra rations of half-cooked maize three times a day for three weeks in early December. During the three weeks the geese almost double their weight and the liver increases in size to between 20 and 30 ounces (600 and 900g). The goose is killed when the

least 300 francs per portion. This truffle develops underground near the roots of oak trees, or occasionally lime or hazel. It prefers limestone soil, and trees which are in poor health. There are several kinds of truffle, but far and away the best of them, the one that the famous French gourmet Brillat-Savarin called 'the black diamond of the kitchen', is the truffle of Périgord. If you want to sample the real thing you should buy only those labelled *truffes de Périgord*. The use of the name is strictly controlled by law. The best place to buy them is in the market places of Périgueux or Sarlat, or in food shops specialising in local products. It used to be the practice to search for truffles using a trained pig, which found them by scent and unearthed them,

FOOD AND DRINK

farmer judges the liver to be at its best.

In Périgord connoisseurs enjoy what is called *foie gras rosé*, or *mi-cuit* (half-cooked), which is the liver so lightly cooked that it is almost raw. Slices are eaten on toast or plain biscuits and accompanied by a good sweet white wine, usually Monbazillac or Sauternes, or by champagne. Visitors who want to take some home can buy it preserved in tins or jars in any good *charcuterie*. It is important to read the label carefully to know exactly what you are buying. Like all luxury products, *foie gras* is often what the French call *truqué*; in other words, fiddled with. Almost every year a producer somewhere in the southwest is accused of marketing *foie gras* which was not exactly what it should have been. The law requires this product to have the ingredients clearly stated somewhere on the

*It may not sound appetising but fat liver (*foie gras*) is a Périgord delicacy*

label. The following are the most usual terms:

Foie gras d'oie (or *de canard*) *au naturel*: pure fattened goose (or duck) liver. It may still have the same label by law so long as it contains not more than 25 per cent of minced pork or veal with the *foie gras*, and the percentage is clearly marked. Such mixtures have a variety of names, the commonest being *pâté* or *terrine*, but whatever it is called, if the words *foie gras* are used, the percentages of other meat must be shown.

If this percentage is high – between 25 and 50 – the word *gras* must be omitted, and the mixture should be called simply *pâté de foie d'oie* or *pâté de foie de canard*. If a product is called *pâté de foie*, it is almost certainly made only from pig's liver.

Any of the above products may have truffles added to them. This will make them more expensive, and the word *truffé* is not likely to be omitted from the label. The percentage of truffles included in the product, which should be shown by law, may be harder to find.

Confit

Another famous Périgord dish is made from the goose or duck, after the liver has been removed. This is called *confit*. The birds are cut into convenient pieces (not usually including the breast, which is set aside for another use), and the joints have most of the fat trimmed off and are then covered in coarse salt for two days. They are then removed and cooked slowly in their own fat until the meat is really well done. Then the pieces are removed and pressed down into an earthenware jar. The remaining fat is refined and then poured over the pieces in the jar to fill it, and the jar is sealed. The *confit* can be taken out and used as required, and keeps in good condition for about six months. The *confit* can be eaten grilled, fried, or cold, but usually it is reheated, surrounded by thinly sliced potatoes which absorb the fat and cook with the heat. *Confit de canard* is found on almost every restaurant menu in Dordogne.

Magret de Canard

Another item very often found on restaurant menus in Dordogne is *magret de canard*. This is the breast meat from a large duck, the rest of which has been used for *confit* or *foie gras*. In restaurants it is normally served roasted and sliced. As with all other meat in France, it will be very much underdone, unless you ask for it *à point* or *bien cuit*.

Cèpes

These mushrooms (pronounced 'sepp') often feature on restaurant menus, either as a dish in themselves, or as an addition to other things, *eg omelette aux cèpes*. They grow in the woodlands of Dordogne and are much used in local cooking, often accompanied by chopped garlic. They belong to the boletus family of mushrooms, and the only one offered in restaurants is the *cèpe de Bordeaux*, which is much the best. They are expensive and add noticeably to the cost of a dish. They are found fresh in autumn, and those on summer menus will have been dried and have less flavour.

Menu French

This is a language of its own, with dozens of specialised terms indicating the way in which different things have been prepared, and dozens more for the kinds of sauces that go with them. Apart from this, some of the raw materials and the other ingredients in Périgord cuisine are unfamiliar. The following brief vocabulary may help.

Offal

Andouillette: a kind of sausage made from the stomach and chitterlings of pigs. Served hot. *Andouille*: a larger version of the same, served cold.

FOOD AND DRINK

Cervelles: brains. Usually *cervelles d'agneau* – lamb's brains.

Gesiers: poultry gizzards cut into small pieces and cooked. Often served warm. Périgord salad contains them.

Ris d'agneau: lamb's sweetbreads. Nothing whatever to do with rice, which is spelt *riz*. Sweetbread with rice, which is possible, would be *ris au riz*.

Poultry and Game

Cassoulet: a stew of goose, kidney beans, mutton, sausages, tomato, etc.

Civet: a stew of rabbit (*lapin*), or hare (*lièvre*), or young wild boar (*marcassin*). Prepared with red wine and some blood in the sauce, like jugged hare. Young hare (*lapereau*) is sometimes offered roast or fried.

Pintade: guinea fowl.

Poulet: roasting chicken; *poule* – boiling fowl; *poussin* – young chicken.

Vegetables

Champignons: the general term for mushrooms. On a menu it means the cultivated version of the ordinary field mushroom. Other mushrooms would be indicated by their proper name, *eg cèpes, truffes, morilles, chanterelles*.

Fish

Bar : sea bass from the Mediterranean. Very good.

Écrevisses: freshwater crayfish. Common in Dordogne; tasty, but needs patience.

Huîtres: oysters. Always fresh and in season in this part of France.

Lamproies: lampreys. Short season in early summer. Well-liked by some; cooked in their own blood and Bordeaux red wine.

Lotte: monkfish. There's a lot about on the cheaper menus.

Loup de Mer: sea bass from the Atlantic.

Quenelles de brochet: small fish cakes made from pike (*brochet*).

Sandre: zander, or pike-perch. One of the best freshwater fish.

Meat

It is important to remember that all meat is habitually undercooked in France, except when it is stewed. When you order meat you will be asked how you want it cooked: *bleu* – lightly cooked on the outside, virtually raw inside; *saignant* – rare, bloody; *à point* – medium; *bien cuit* – well done (you'll be lucky).

Jambon: ham. The boiled, boned York ham is *jambon blanc* or *jambon de Paris*, but in Dordogne you are most likely to find *jambon de campagne*. This is ham prepared by salting for several weeks, thorough rinsing, and air-drying for several months. Every farmer's wife has her own way of doing it, and the result can vary from a close imitation to boot leather to something more like Parma ham.

Desserts

Clafoutis: a moist cake sunk with cherries.

Coulis: a liquid purée of fresh fruit, usually raspberries or strawberries, often served with its own fruit or ice cream to strengthen the flavour.

Noix: always means walnuts on a

FOOD AND DRINK

Périgord menu. Walnut cakes are common in Dordogne, rare further south.

Tourtière: popular in the southwest, including Dordogne. A tart of wafer-thin pastry, flavoured with Armagnac, and filled with prunes, or apples (when it may be called *croustade*).

Wine

Dordogne produces red and rosé wines, and both sweet and dry whites.

Those red wines with an AOC label (*Appellation Contrôlée d'Origine*) are Bergerac, Côtes de Bergerac, and Pécharmant. The best of these is generally reckoned to be Pécharmant. It is not made in large quantities and rarely reaches the shelves of the supermarkets, but is found on the wine lists of better restaurants in Dordogne. It is a wine which should be at least four years old when drunk. The normal Bergerac reds contain little tannin and can be drunk quite young. At 12 to 20 francs a bottle they represent good value.

The dry white wines of Bergerac and Montravel go well with fish. Some of them, made from the Sauvignon grape, are particularly good value at about 15 francs a bottle.

The finest of the wines produced in Dordogne is the luscious, sweet Monbazillac. In good years it rivals the better Sauternes and is one of the world's great sweet white wines. Like Sauternes, it is made largely from the Semillon grape, harvested very late in the year, when the grapes are overripe

Pécharmant is generally judged to be the best of Bergerac's good quality red wines

and have the 'noble rot'. Local people drink it as an aperitif, and it is the wine they prefer with *foie gras*. It also goes well with melon and with fruit desserts. The Bergerac rosés are light and dry, at their best chilled on a hot summer day. *Crême de noix*, *eau de noix*, and *brou de noix* are just some of the liqueurs, etc, made from walnuts. In ordinary country hotels and restaurants it is always a sound idea to take the *Cuvée du Patron*, the house wine. These hotels depend on regular commercial business throughout the year and they would not get it, unless their wine was reliable. Otherwise expect to pay three to four times the hypermarket price for decent wines.

ACCOMMODATION

Accommodation in Dordogne is divided between hotels, camp sites and *gîtes ruraux*, which could be described as 'country cottages'.

Hotels

Nowadays there are two completely different kinds of hotel in France: the traditional and the modern. The traditional hotels are family-run, have bedrooms with heavily flowered wallpaper and mostly large double beds, dining rooms with beams and cases of stuffed animals, and bathrooms which, though quite modern, have often been made by taking a corner of a large bedroom. Most of the Logis de France, Auberges de France and France Accueil are of this type, and in all these family hotels you will be made welcome by the proprietors themselves. Often Mum looks after the running of the place, and Dad is the chef.

In the past 10 years or so, a number of hotel chains have been started and have rapidly expanded. Among them are Novotel, Ibis, Climat, Campanile, Sofitel and Mercure. These hotels are aimed at the business as well as the holiday market, and are often sited near the industrial zones of towns, or near airports. They have the advantage that they are not used by business men at weekends, so that tourists can often find a room at that time, sometimes at a discounted rate. Novotel do not charge for children under 12 who sleep in their parents' room. They are impersonal and predictable, in as much as one is very like another. You are not likely to see the manager unless you have a serious complaint, which is unlikely.

Whichever type of hotel you prefer, it is important in the holiday season to book ahead. The time has passed when it was possible to be sure of finding a room for the night in the first hotel that took your fancy. You could be lucky, but it is unlikely. So reserve in advance, even if it is only on the morning of the same day, and remember that family hotels with a restaurant expect you to take dinner, and are much more likely to have a room if you say you will have a meal. Room and all meals, *ie* full board (or *pension*) terms are offered for a stay of three days or more. Half board or *demi-pension* (room, breakfast and one meal) terms are usually available. Rooms in older hotels vary in size and amenities: some do not have baths, for example, and the price varies accordingly. This should be taken into account when you note the classification of the hotel, which can vary from Tourist upwards so that a one-star hotel may well have some rooms which are better than some rooms in a two-star, and the same applies all the way up the scale. Prices in French hotels are for the room and not per person. A double room let to one person may not be reduced in price; however, a double room is generally cheaper than two separate rooms. For a third bed in a room you will only be charged around an extra 30 per cent.

ACCOMMODATION

A traditional family hotel: Hôtel Cro-Magnon, Les Eyzies-de-Tayac

It is a general rule in France that everyone is expected to look after their own interests. When you arrive at a hotel, they will expect you to ask to see the room, and to ask for something different if it does not suit you. In principle they like to book up their less good rooms first, so just check that you have not been given one next to the lift, or on the noisy street side when, on the other side of the corridor, the rooms overlook a peaceful garden.

All this can apply even in the modern chains, though, because the rooms and the prices are standardised within the hotel, the room itself is likely to be acceptable.

A number of the older hotels, although independently owned, belong to marketing organisations such as Logis de France, Mapotel, or Inter-Hotel. These organisations expect certain standards to be maintained in return for their marketing services. Clearly, they could not survive for long by marketing rotten hotels. Mapotel and Inter-Hotel tend to represent medium-sized hotels in towns, and are of good average standard. Like hotel chains they operate a central booking service. Logis de France specialise in small hotels, equivalent to the one-, two- or some three-star hotels, and nearly always in country situations.

Hotels belonging to Logis de France are recognised by a distinctive sign representing an old brick hearth. A free guide of hotels under the direction of Logis de France and Auberges de France is available from the French Government Tourist Offices. Bookings are made direct with individual hotels.

ACCOMMODATION

Campsites

There are said to be more than 150 campsites in Dordogne, with more than 20 within easy reach of Sarlat. As everywhere else in France, they vary from the rough and ready, where the guy-ropes of tents may overlap each other, to four-star luxury with all the latest amenities. You will find some sites in the grounds of romantic châteaux. Well appointed, these sites have all been credited with three or four stars, and are organised by **Castels et Camping-Caravanning**, BP 301, 56008 Vannes (tel: 97 42 55 83; fax: 97 47 50 72). All graded sites must display their official classification, site regulations, capacity and current charges at the site entrance.

Some, mostly municipal and sites not usually of the highest quality, stay open all year, but many campsites close in early September, as soon as French children have returned to school. Outside July and August, you can drive into those good camps which are still open and choose your own position from the many that will be free. If you want to get into a good site during the high season, it is essential to book ahead. If you plan a camping holiday, it is best to try and arrange it through a tour operator. The French Government Tourist Office can supply information of reputable tour operators or a list of sites to enable you to book direct, while local tourist information offices can supply more detailed information about sites in their locality.

Camping information can also be obtained from many Total petrol service stations in France. During July and August if you want to know which sites in Dordogne have space you should telephone 53 50 79 80. The following is a brief selection of some of the better sites:

Beau Rivage, La Roque-Gageac, 24250 Domme (tel: 53 28 32 05). Open all year. This site is 2 miles (4km) from La Roque-Gageac village, just across the river from Domme off the D703. Beside the Dordogne.

Cantegrel, Rouffignac, 24580 Rouffignac-St Cernin (tel: 53 05 48 30). Pleasant site 1 mile (1.5km) north of Rouffignac, via D31. Must reserve in high season.

Étang de Moulinal, Biron, 24540 Monpazier (tel: 53 40 84 60). Large, but nice camp beside a small lake. One mile (1.5km) from village of Lacapelle-Biron by road to Villeréal.

La Fôret, Pezuls, 24510 Ste-Alvère (tel: 53 22 71 69). Well-equipped site, with pool and tennis courts, on the D703.
Les Granges, 24250 Groléjac en Périgord (tel: 53 28 11 15). Off the D704 Sarlat-Gourdon road. Signposted in Groléjac village (turn off D704, towards Domme).
Le Moulin de David, Gaugeac, 24250 Monpazier (tel: 53 22 65 25). Two miles (3km) outside Monpazier by D2 towards Villeréal.
Le Moulin du Roch, route des Eyzies, St Andre d'Allas, 24200 Sarlat. Six miles (10km) north D6, west by D47 (tel: 53 59 20 27). Castel et Camping-Caravanning site.
Les Ormes, St Étienne de Villeréal, 47210 Villeréal (tel: 53 36 60 26). Half a mile (1km) south of Villeréal, off D255.

Bargaining at Sarlat market

Attractive site just over the border, in Lot-et-Garonne.
La Palombière, St Nathalène, 24200 Sarlat. Five and a half miles northeast, by D47 (tel: 53 59 42 34). Well-equipped modern camp.
Le Paradis, St-Léon-sur-Vézère, 24290 Montignac (tel: 53 50 72 64). Off D706, halfway between Les Eyzies and Montignac, so well-placed for exploring Vézère valley.
Les Perrières, 24200 Sarlat (tel: 53 59 05 84). Spacious site, situated only half a mile (1km) outside town.

Country Cottages
One of the most enjoyable ways of spending a holiday in Dordogne is to rent your own cottage. The cottages, which are called *gîtes ruraux* in French, or *gîtes* for short, are often situated on farms. Some may even be in the modernised outbuildings of farmhouses. They vary in size from those for two people up to houses which will take as many as 10 in comfort.
There are also a number of holiday villages offering accommodation in log cabins or chalets. Some of these villages are attractively laid out and are situated on lakesides with swimming and boating facilities. For local information, help and advice on accommodation contact the Syndicats d'Initiative in larger towns.
There are many tour operators offering holidays in Dordogne, including hotels, self-catering country cottages and camping and caravanning. Contact the French Government Tourist Office for information.

SHOPPING

Opening Hours

Food shops normally open at 08.00 and close at 12.30hrs, and are open again from 16.00 until 19.00hrs or later, including Saturdays. They are closed on Mondays, at least in the morning, though some open in the afternoon. Some food shops open on Sunday mornings from 09.00hrs to midday. Bakers open earlier in the mornings, and are generally open on Sunday mornings.

Most other shops are open from 09.00hrs (some earlier) to noon, and from 14.00 to 18.00hrs (some later). Most are closed on Sundays and all day Monday. Hypermarkets and supermarkets typically open at 09.00 until 12.30hrs and from 15.00 to 19.00 or 20.00hrs. Hours vary, but are posted outside each hypermarket, so note them when you arrive at a place where you are going to stay. Some have cafeterias (*Mammouth*, for example) and, if so, do not close for lunch. Most have one late-night shopping day, usually Friday.and may close on Monday mornings.

Shops for Tourists

Broadly speaking, visiting shoppers divide into those who are self-caterers staying on campsites or in rented cottages, who need to shop almost every day, and those in hotels who shop only for souvenirs, etc. Self-caterers are well advised to shop in hypermarkets, where prices are competitive and clearly marked on every item, and where everything they are likely to need for the household can be obtained under one roof. French butchers (*boucheries*) joint differently, and prepare the meat so that there is very little waste. Lamb, all poultry, veal and offal are all first-class. Beef is less good. Fish, fruit and fresh vegetables are all excellent.

Dordogne shops can be as attractive as the products they sell: this bookshop is in Périgueux

Markets

Do not expect to find bargains of any kind in markets, though shopping in them may be much more fun. You may find an item being sold more cheaply than in a shop you know, but if you look carefully, you will probably find that it is available cheaply at some shops, too.

Souvenirs

Baskets: these come in all shapes and sizes and for all kinds of specialist purposes, and are beautifully made by hand.

Cooking utensils: from small gadgets for the kitchen not easily found outside France – electric powered oyster knives for example – up to cast-iron cooking pots and copper pans for jam-making.

Food: *pâté de foie gras* and other local products (see **Food and Drink** section), in hermetically sealed jars or tins, are best bought in Sarlat (Delpeyrat is a good supplier) or Périgueux, or Bergerac. Fruit such as plums, prunes, peaches, cherries, etc, bottled in *eau de vie* or Armagnac, keeps a long time, even after being opened. Dordogne is a great area for hunting and fishing, and every town has at least one tackle shop, with specialised clothes and equipment of all kinds at prices which are bound to be competitive.

Wine: most people take some back, and it is a bargain, especially when bought in hypermarkets.

WEATHER AND WHEN TO GO

The holiday season in Dordogne starts in April and ends in October. There is not a lot of point in going outside these dates, as most of the sights, and many of the hotels and restaurants, are closed. A very high percentage of visitors arrive July and August. Summers in Dordogne are sunny and can be hot at any time from June to the end of September, and very hot in July and August, when shade temperatures often reach 30°C (90°F). In some summers, hot weather is interrupted by violent storms with heavy rainfall, but there are also summers with no storms. Summer is often prolonged right through October, and with the autumnal tints in the woodlands this can be an enjoyable time for those who like the outdoor life and not too much heat.

If you want to avoid crowds when sightseeing, June and September are the best months, and there is still quite a lot open until mid-October.

There are a lot of caves in Dordogne, and caves are cold. There can be as much as 17°C (30°F) difference between an outside temperature and the depths of a cave, so take a pullover for underground. Some people may also appreciate something warm in the air-conditioned hypermarkets in the height of summer. It is possible to take meals out of doors all summer, but evenings in early May and late September can be fresh, and something woollen may be welcome.

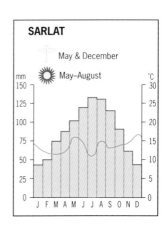

SARLAT

May & December

mm / May–August / °C

CULTURE, ENTERTAINMENT AND NIGHTLIFE

Dordogne is not the place to go for riotous entertainment. Peace and quiet is a major characteristic of the region. Having said that, there is plenty going on during the summer season, both of a permanent and an occasional nature.

Cinema is still a popular art form in France: attendances are on the increase and most towns of any size have a cinema, often with a choice of films. There are several cinemas in Périgueux and Bergerac. Admission is about 40 francs.

Discos: there are more than you might expect, and many are open all year round. They are often in the coutryside, a few miles outside towns, where there are no neighbours to annoy. They are mostly used by local French people, and tend to cater for a particular type of clientele – some for teenagers, some for young people, some for older people who like the *balmusette* (accordion) music and dancing – the word *retro* (old-time) refers to this sort of club – and there are some for homosexuals in some large towns. The best thing to do is to seek local advice, explaining the sort of club you prefer. The police keep an eye on these clubs and most of them are well run. The usual entrance fee is about 70 francs, which includes a drink.

Music and Theatre: music and theatre festivals are arranged in different places in Périgord every summer. Sarlat always has one. Details can be obtained from local Syndicats d'Initiative.

Fireworks: the French like fireworks, and there are always some good displays during the summer, notably on 14 July and 15 August.

Most towns have dances and festivities on Midsummer Night, the Fête de St Jean.

HOW TO BE A LOCAL

If you want to behave like a local inhabitant while you are in Dordogne, you should begin by getting up early; about 06.30hrs is the usual time. Life in southern France starts early: most shops and many offices are open by 08.00hrs (hypermarkets 09.00hrs). For breakfast you will have coffee and bread, perhaps croissants, but nothing else. Whatever you decide to do, you will stop sharp at noon for lunch, and you will not be available, except on the telephone, for another two hours. (This is a good rule even if you are eating out – by 12.30hrs all the best tables and some of the dishes will have gone.)

This lunch will be the main meal of the day. You will not take a morning snack nor afternoon tea. Early in the evening, you will have a light meal – soup and bread, and perhaps a boiled egg or a salad. You will be in bed at a very reasonable hour. If you eat out, it is likely to be at lunchtime, particularly on Sunday, and with relatives rather than friends. Sunday is also the day for visiting friends and relatives at home, and you take with you not a bottle of wine or a bunch of flowers, but a

Buy your **pain** *from the* **boulangerie**
if you want to be a local

gâteau from the pâtisserie, all
open on Sunday mornings.
As a relaxation, and if you can
find someone ready to show you
how, you will play *boules* in the
village square in the company of
retired senior citizens and the
unemployed, or pretend you
are a local by sitting outside the
café watching the tourists and
the rest of the world go by.
If there is a local village fête, you
will be welcome. There is
usually music and dancing, and
a buffet, and a lottery in which
you can, if you are one of the
lucky ones, win a pig, or goose,
or something else edible.

PERSONAL PRIORITIES

Here, as everywhere else in
France, all attitudes relating to
sex are those of a live and let-
live society. Homosexuals of
both sexes are far less common
than in big cities. On the other
hand, young couples who enjoy
a third partner are not rare. The
majority of French people are
formal and well behaved on the
whole, unless encouraged to be
otherwise.
Women travelling alone who
behave sensibly will be as safe
here as anywhere in the world.
Some discos and night clubs
offer free admission to
unaccompanied women, but
taking advantage of this is
inadvisable, as is visiting any
unfamiliar club with casual
acquaintances and then
accepting 'a lift home' with
unknown drivers who have had
too much to drink. The toll of
young people killed in car
accidents late at night in France
is tragic. So, if you want to go to
a night club or disco, go in a
group with people you know
well, and make sure you can
arrange your own transport.
Hitch-hiking is not advised. Most
French drivers never give lifts,
and hitch-hikers travelling alone
are taking a real risk.

CHILDREN

Facilities do vary from place to place so, wherever you are staying, do ask at the nearest Office de Tourisme or Syndicat d'Initiative about the activities which interest you. Here are some of the more usual amenities.

Boating: on most rivers, canoes and kayaks can be hired by the day or the week. At Bergerac, Beynac and Trémolat short boat trips on the Dordogne, using the traditional trading craft of the river – the shallow draft barges called *gabardes* – are available.

Caves: children may well be more impressed by those with natural stalactite and crystalline formations and dramatic lighting effects, than with those with cave paintings, which are in other respects more ordinary.

Cycling: bicycles may be hired in many places, but there never seem to be enough to go round, so ask early.

Day trips: if you are staying put in your own rented cottage or on a camp site, rather than touring, there are plenty of things likely to interest children on day trips: visits to caves, museums, zoos, castles, etc. One special trip from Périgord Noir would be to the Gouffre de Padirac, in the Lot department, where you can take a boat trip on an underground lake. Reached via Souillac and Rocamadour, it is also a very picturesque drive.

Fishing: can be arranged in lakes or rivers, but is rather expensive for short stays.

Museums: among the best for children are the Museum of

Prehistory at Les Eyzies, the Cro-Magnon Centre at Le Thot, and the Museum of Medieval Warfare at the Château de Castelnaud.

Riding: there are many centres for horse-riding (called *Équitation* in French) throughout Dordogne, either by the hour or on week-long accompanied pony-treks. The Sports and Leisure Centre at Rouffiac in Périgord Vert offers three-day beginners' courses in riding or windsurfing, or four-day courses in riding plus another activity – archery, windsurfing, canoeing or rock climbing – with accommodation and meals, if required.

Walking: there are many miles of signposted footpaths through the woods and over the hills,

Leisure in a historical setting: the Roman arena in Périgueux

ideal for family rambles and birdwatching, etc. In some places it is possible to hire horse-drawn caravans for the weekend. These travel at walking pace, and the younger or less keen walkers can rest aboard when they feel like it.
Windsurfing: possible in many places, with instruction. See under **Riding**.
Zoos and safari parks: there are several. There are also wild animals in the Cro-Magnon Centre at Le Thot.

TIGHT BUDGET

If you are buying your own food and self-catering you will find the most competitive prices in the large hypermarkets. Otherwise it pays to shop around before buying, as prices vary between shops of the same kind. In restaurants, tailor the meal to match your appetite. If you are hungry, it will pay you to take a menu with several courses, rather than to eat *à la carte*. But if you are not hungry, you may well find a single dish *à la carte* which is cheaper than the cheapest menu. You are not obliged to take more.
Remember that it is not unusual to find the cheaper menus, say from 60 francs, where several of the dishes offered have an extra charge which puts the price up by another 10 francs, or more. If you decide to eat *à la carte*, do not forget that the cheese and dessert courses are often relatively expensive.
Coffee is always an extra, and can increase the bill noticeably if several people are dining. In some restaurants wine is still complimentary, to the equivalent of two or three glasses. If not, you will save money by taking the *vin du patron*, the house wine. Wines on the wine list will cost from two-and-a-half to four times what exactly the same will cost in the hypermarket. Some cheaper wines can even be marked up to six times their retail value.
Fuel is always pretty expensive in this area, but varies quite a lot from one place to another. It is invariably most expensive on the autoroutes, and cheapest at the hypermarket, many of which have their own fuel station. It is a good idea to take some oil with you as it is expensive in France.

SPECIAL EVENTS AND FESTIVALS

Music and theatre festivals and sporting events of all kinds take place all over Dordogne throughout the June to September season. They vary from year to year. Some are annual events but the dates vary. Full information from the local Syndicats d'Initiative (also see **Culture, Entertainment and Nightlife**, page 110).

SPORT

Dordogne is an ideal setting for sport and outdoor activities of all kinds. There are hundreds of miles of signposted footpaths through forests and magnificent countryside. Horse-riding and pony-trekking are available in many different centres, some

Dordogne's glorious scenery can make swimming and boating ideal

with accommodation. Canoes or kayaks can be rented for day outings or longer expeditions on a number of rivers. There is safe swimming from many lake or river beaches, and most towns have a municipal swimming pool. Both trout and coarse fishing are possible, but can be expensive, as the purchase of an annual fishing card is required, and there are no short-stay arrangements. Much the same applies to tennis. Every town and most villages have excellent tennis courts, but they have an annual membership fee, and no special arrangements for visitors. There are golf courses which can be used by visitors on the payment of green fees. Bicycles can be hired in most centres and from railway stations.

Visitors should ask at the local Syndicats d'Initiative for details of the sport or activity which interests them.

DIRECTORY

Contents

Arriving

There are direct flights from most European cities, including London, to Bordeaux (75 miles (120km) from Périgueux and the nearest airport for Dordogne), for which Air France is the main carrier. Bordeaux is only one hour by plane from Paris; Air Inter operate a daily service there. The only direct internal air service is Air Littoral, which flies to Périgueux three times a day and twice on Saturdays and Sundays; and to Bergerac three times a day and once on Saturdays and Sundays.

The great majority of tourists go to Dordogne by car. Those coming from the eastern Channel ports would normally route themselves via or around Paris to Orléans, and down the N20 to Limoges, and change there to the N21 to Périgueux. From the western Channel ports, a variety of routes is possible as far as Poitiers, where the direct route is the N10 to Angoulême, and from there the D939 to Périgueux. Those travellers using Motorail (information from French Government Tourist Office) will

arrive at Brive-la-Gallarde, and take the N89 towards Périgueux or D60 towards Sarlat and the Périgord Noir.

It is possible to combine the speed of air travel with the flexibility of rail travel. Air France and French Railways offer a bargain price ticket from airports in Britain and Ireland to Paris, from where you continue your journey by train. For Périgueux it is necessary to change trains at Limoges or Brive-la-Gaillarde.

There is a rail service from Paris (Austerlitz) to Agen with stops in Dordogne at Thiviers, Périgueux and Le Buisson (about 10½ miles/17km from Les Eyzies). The journey takes about seven hours during the day, and about nine by the stopping train at night.

Travel by air, rail or bus within Dordogne is either non-existent or completely impractical. This is why well over 90 per cent of travellers come to Dordogne by car.

Camping see
Accommodation, page 106, for a list of campsites.

DIRECTORY

There are more than 150 campsites in Dordogne; in the high season it is essential to book ahead. Motorists may sometimes see notices which say *Camping à la Ferme*. This means that the farmer will allow tents to be pitched on his land, and *may* accept a caravan. Although the standards will almost certainly be pretty basic.

Crime

This is not something which visitors need worry about in Dordogne, but, all the same, do not leave valuables in unlocked cars. Any loss or theft should be reported to the nearest *commissariat de police* or *gendarmerie*.

Customs

Visitors to France, as a general rule, may *temporarily* import personal articles duty-free, providing they are considered as being in use and in keeping with the personal status of the importer.

The allowances for duty and tax-<u>free</u> goods brought into France are:
Spirits (over 22 per cent vol)
   1 litre
    or
Alcoholic drink (not over 22 per cent vol)
   2 litres
    plus
Still table wine
   2 litres
Cigarettes 200
   (400 for non-Europeans)
Cigarillos 100
   (200 for non-Europeans)
Cigars 50
   (100 for non-Europeans)
Tobacco 250g
   (500g for non-Europeans)
Perfume 60ml
Toilet water 250ml
Other goods
up to the value of 300 francs per person (150 francs per person under 15 years of age) from a non-European Union (EU)

You may have trouble getting this much wine through customs...

country, and 2,400 francs per person (620 francs per person under 15 years of age) from an EU country.

Larger amounts of the above goods may be brought into France if obtained duty and tax-paid from countries in the EU. People under 17 years of age are not entitled to duty and tax-free allowances in respect of alcohol and tobacco.

Visitors to France entering from an EU country may also import duty-free 1kg of coffee (or 450g of coffee extract) and 250g of tea (or 80g of tea extract); a reduced allowance applies if bought duty-free.

There are no restrictions on the import of foreign or French currency, but amounts exceeding 50,000 francs should be declared on a currency declaration form upon arrival.

Exportation. What you may take out of France depends upon the import regulations of the country of your destination, which you should consult before leaving.

Driving

Police and gendarmes are sticklers for documents, and will ask to see them for whatever reason you may have been stopped. For tourists this means a valid passport, a full valid national driving licence and the car's registration document and insurance. If it is a borrowed car, they will want to see a written permit from the owner for you to use it. An international distinguishing sign, with the letter(s) of the country of the car's registration, should also be displayed at the rear of the car.

Car lights: for cars brought into France from Britain and Eire, headlights should be adjusted for driving on the right-hand side of the road to avoid dazzling oncoming drivers. This is achieved by fitting headlamp converters (PVC mask sheets) or beam deflectors (clip-on lenses), obtainable before you leave from most good motor accessory shops.

French registered vehicles are equipped with headlights that show a yellow beam, and although this is not compulsory for visiting motorists, they are advised to comply. Beam deflectors can be purchased with yellow lenses; otherwise, a yellow 'lacquer' needs to be applied to the headlamp glass. In addition, it is recommended that motorists have a complete spare-bulb kit for their vehicle, for it is an offence not to be able to replace a faulty bulb when you are requested to do so by the police.

Fuel: there is no standard price for fuel in France. It goes up and down like a yo-yo from garage to garage, and from week to week. It is always most expensive on the autoroutes. Most cars run on *sans plomb* (unleaded) fuel, but some use *Super* (high octane) or *Essence* (low octane), or Diesel. In Dordogne, many petrol stations are closed all day on Sundays, so fill up if you intend driving at these times. If you want a full tank ask for *Le plein, s'il vous plaît*. The minimum amount of petrol which may be purchased at a station is normally five litres (just over one gallon).

Roads: during July and August, especially at weekends, traffic on main roads is likely to be very heavy. Alternative, less congested routes are signposted by emerald green arrows. Also, a free road map showing marked alternative routes is available from service stations displaying the *Bison Futé* sign (a Red Indian chief in full war bonnet). It is usually advantageous to follow these routes, for, although you cannot be absolutely sure of gaining time, the quieter secondary roads generally provide the visitor with a more relaxing and scenic drive.

Road signs: France uses the normal international road signs, plus a few of its own. *Chaussée déformée* means a badly uneven road surface for the distance named. *Chantier* or *Travaux* means road works. *Chantier mobile* means road works with a large machine, *eg* a tar spreader, moving about. *Fauchage* means grass verges are being cut by machine.

A peculiarity of driving in France *in built-up areas* is the rule of giving way to traffic coming from the right (*priorité à droite*), including even small side-turnings. The exception is on junctions with signs bearing the words *Vous n'avez pas la priorité* or *Cédez le Passage*. *Outside built-up areas*, however, all main roads of any importance have right of way. This is indicated by one of three possible signs on the road:

- A red-bordered triangle surrounding a black cross on a white background with the words *Passage Protégé* underneath.
- A red-bordered triangle with

a pointed black upright with a horizontal bar on a white background.

- A yellow diamond within a white diamond. (The yellow diamond crossed out means 'you no longer have priority').

Watch for road markings – do not cross a solid white or yellow line marked on the centre of the road.

Look out carefully, too, for traffic lights; they are dim and sometimes high above the middle of the road, and can easily be missed. A flashing amber light warns that the intersection or junction is particularly dangerous; a flashing red light indicates no entry.

Car Rental: expensive, particularly from well-known car rental firms (*location de voitures*), but in towns there is often a reliable local firm, with

Bergerac, which today has a population of 27,000, is one of the main centres of Périgord Blanc

less choice of car model but cheaper rates.

The minimum age to hire a car is 18, but most firms set the limit at 21–23 years.

Speeding: the police are much stricter about this, and about drink/driving, than they were a few years ago. The minimum fine for simple speeding is 1,300 francs, and can be much more (up to 30,000 for drink/driving). Fines must be paid in cash on the spot.

The speed limit in built-up areas is 50kph (31mph), even in apparently deserted villages. (The beginning of a built-up area is marked by a sign with the place name in black or blue letters on a light background; the end by the same sign with a red line diagonally across it.)

Outside built-up areas on normal roads, the limits are 90kph (56mph); on dual-carriageways, 110kph (68mph). There are no motorways in Dordogne. In wet weather, speed limits are reduced outside built-up areas to 80kph (49mph); on dual-carriageways, 90kph (56mph). These limits also apply to cars towing a caravan. If you have held a full driving licence for less than one year, you must not exceed 90kph (56mph) or any lower signposted limit when driving in France. Although there is no set *minimum* speed limit (except on motorways), it can be an offence in France to travel at so slow a speed, without good reason, as to obstruct traffic flow.

Breakdowns: there are emergency phones at 12½ mile (20km) intervals on some roads, but elsewhere you have to find one. They occur away from towns and villages on the main N roads, on yellow, orange or red posts marked with a telephone and 'SOS'. Emergency phones are connected direct to the local police station – the police will contact a garage for you. Otherwise you are advised to seek local assistance, as at the present time there is no nationwide road assistance service in France. However, towing and on-the-spot repairs can be made by local garages, but always ask for an estimate first. Motorists are advised to take out some form of internationally valid breakdown insurance such as the Automobile Association's Five-star service before leaving home for Dordogne.

DIRECTORY

Electricity

The electricity supply is generally 220 volts so transformers are not normally required. Plugs are generally of the 2 'round' pin type (or occasionally 3 round pins). Useful adaptors to convert electrical appliances are best bought from electrical stores before leaving home.

Embassies and Consulates

None in Dordogne. Nearest British Consulate is at 353 Boulevard Président Wilson, Bordeaux (tel: 56 42 34 13). Americans, Canadians and Australians should contact their respective Embassies in Paris:
US: 2 Avenue Gabriel, 75382 Paris Cedex 08 (tel: 42 96 12 02).
Canada: 35 Avenue Mantaigne, 75008 Paris Cedex 08 (tel: 47 23 01 01).
Australia: 4 Rue Jean Rey, 75724 Paris Cedex 15 (tel: 40 59 33 00).

Emergency Telephone Numbers

The usual emergency numbers are 17 for the police, 18 for the fire brigade (*pompiers*), who deal with most things – wasp nests, trapped animals, etc – except crime. Emergency medical aid is available through SAMV, whose number varies from locality to locality but can be found on Page 1 of the local telephone directory (*l'annuaire*).

Entertainment see Culture, Entertainment and Nightlife, page 110.

Make use of the local Offices de Tourisme, and Syndicats d'Initiative, who will have full information on any sports, music, drama, fireworks, or other activities for that area.

Entry Formalities

All visitors to France should be in possession of a valid, up-to-date national passport. British Nationals need only a British Passport. Irish Citizens too need only their passport. For visitors resident outside of the European Union (including the United States, Canada and Australia), a visa is required. Information on visa formalities is available from the nearest French Consulate.

Health

No vaccinations advised, no formalities. French doctors and medical services are very good. A charge is made for a visit to the doctor at his surgery – a higher rate if he comes to you. Doctors who belong to the French social security system (*médecins conventionnés*) charge the least. Medical emergencies are covered by normal holiday insurance (either private or Tour Operators'), but a simple visit to a doctor may not be. Britain has a reciprocal health agreement with France under which visitors can obtain *urgently* needed medical treatment at a reduced cost. A certificate of entitlement (form *E111*) is issued by the Department of Health (residents of Eire must apply to their Regional Health Board), which must be produced to obtain concessionary treatment. You will be entitled to have your medical costs defrayed at levels from 70 per cent to 80 per cent.

*Stepping out in traditional
Dordogne folk costume*

Charges are refunded at the
local Sickness Insurance Office
(*Caisse Primaires d'Assurance-
Maladie*). Any balance should
be covered by personal health
insurance. The forms and
prescriptions which the doctor
and chemist give you should be
taken to the *Caisse Primaires
d'Assurance-Maladie* – the
doctor will have the address,
and you will eventually get a
part-refund.

Holidays
French public holidays on which
banks and most shops are
closed are:
1 January (New Year's Day);
Easter Sunday and Monday;
1 May (Labour Day);
Ascension Day;
VE Day;
Whit Sunday and Monday;
14 July (Bastille Day);
15 August (Assumption Day);
1 November (All Saint's Day);
11 November (Armistice Day);
25 December (Christmas Day).

Lost Property
Not much to do about this. The
gendarmerie are likely to shrug
and tell you they have better
things to do.
Railway stations and Town Halls
have an *Objets Trouvés* (Things
Found) section.

Media
English language radio
broadcasts of the BBC World
Service can be picked up on
1296KHz (231m); 648KHz
(463m); or 198KHz (1515m),
with world news on the hour.
English language newspapers
are obtainable at newsagents in
the larger towns, and often in
only one of them. An English
language monthly newspaper,
The News, is published from
Eymet in Dordogne and
circulates widely. It covers local
and national problems.

DIRECTORY

Money Matters

The unit of currency is the franc, divided into 100 centimes. Denominations of banknotes are: 20, 50, 100, 200 and 500; standard coins are 1, 2, 10 and 50 francs, and 5, 10, 20 and 50 centimes.

Banks work on a five-day week, and those which are closed on Mondays are open all day Saturdays, and vice versa, so that it is always possible to find a bank open, except on Sundays. Opening hours vary but are approximately 09.00hrs–noon and 14.00–17.00hrs. Banks close at midday on the day before a national holiday and all day on Monday if the holiday falls on a Tuesday.

Changing Money: not all branches deal with foreign exchange, so look for the sign *change* outside the bank. Eurocheques, travellers' cheques, Access and Visa cards, American Express, *Carte Bleue* and Diners Club are widely accepted in hotels and restaurants. Some are accepted in many petrol stations, but not in all hypermarkets. When paying by credit card, check the amount on the receipt. There is no decimal point shown between francs and centimes. Except in emergencies, do not change money in hotels; the rate is always poor.

Opening Times

For shops see **Shopping**, page 108.

Businesses: 09.00 (sometimes earlier) to 18.00hrs (sometimes later) with a strict two-hour lunch break from noon to 14.00hrs.

Sunflowers near Bergerac

Banks: approximately 09.00hrs–noon and 14.00–17.00hrs.

Museums, etc: where a museum or a château or other building is owned by the state or department, it is likely to be closed on Tuesdays. Municipal buildings, etc, are closed on Mondays, and may close in the winter. This means almost all museums and a fair number of châteaux. Some sites are closed for the lunch break, normally two hours. Some private sites are open every day of the week, and in high season, all day. Admission prices vary, but, as an indication, fees for national museums average 10 to 25 francs; with a 50 per cent reduction on Sundays. Municipal museums, however, offer free admission to their permanent collections.

Pharmacist

Pharmacies are recognisable by the sign of a green cross.

Pharmacists in France have basic medical training, can administer first-aid and are used to giving sensible advice for everyday ailments. They are normally open six days a week, and take it in turns to be the *Pharmacie de Garde, ie*, the one which, by law, must be open on Sunday when the others are closed. The address of the one which is open is posted on the door of those which are closed, published in the local newspaper, or can be obtained from the local gendarmerie.

Places of Worship
There are Protestant churches throughout Dordogne, one of the most important Huguenot areas in France. Enquire locally. Times of Catholic mass vary, as one priest may officiate in two or three villages. Enquire locally.

Police
The police, who are civil servants, are responsible for law and order in the towns. In the country, this is the responsibility of the gendarmes, who are attached to the army. Policing the roads is divided between them, though motor cycle police are normally police, not gendarmes. Police and gendarmes wear blue uniforms; police wear military-style caps, and gerdarmes wear *képis*. They are both inclined to be indulgent towards tourists, except over serious matters. It is a courtesy to know the difference between them, but, as far as visitors are concerned, one is as bad or as good as the other. In the deep country there is also an officer known as a *garde champêtre*, who is a kind of maid-of-all-work village policeman.

Post Office
These carry the sign of a blue bird or the initials 'PTT'. Larger post offices are normally open from 08.00 to 17.00 or 18.00hrs Monday to Friday, and do not close for lunch. Smaller ones may close for lunch, but if they stay open they then normally close earlier. Post offices also open 08.00hrs to noon on Saturdays. You can buy stamps at any position in the post office, or at any tobacconist; a book of stamps is called a *carnet de timbres*. There are telephone booths in most post offices. You ask at the counter for a line, the call is registered electronically and you pay at the counter. There are sets of directories for the whole of France in main post offices, and the Yellow Pages can be a help in finding any service you may need. Through the *poste restante* system you

DIRECTORY

can be contacted while in France. If you expect mail, call with your passport at the main post office of the town where you are staying.

Public Transport

Air: there are airports in

Buses do exist in Dordogne, but it is easier to find other ways of getting around the area

Bergerac and Périgueux for French internal flights, but except for the longest distances they are less efficient than the railways (see **Arriving**, page 115).

Rail: very good between major towns, but in Dordogne hardly worth bothering about. By the time you have driven to a station you may well feel that it would have been better to drive the whole way. But if you are

leaving Dordogne for some other part of France, ask for advantageous tickets which exist for senior citizens and young travellers.

Buses: attempting to travel around by bus is best forgotten in Dordogne. There are once-a-day each-way services between key places, and once- or twice-a-week services from villages to towns for market days, and the buses which take children to and from school, and that's it. In the countryside of France, transport means motor car, bicycle or walking.

Senior Citizens and Student Travel

Young people under 26 and senior citizens can obtain advantageous rates for rail travel on some trains to or from Dordogne. Details can be obtained from any French railway station.

Telephones

Telephone numbers outside France are obtained by dialling 19, waiting for a new tone, then dialling the code of the country concerned, then the area code (omitting the first zero), followed by the telephone number in that country.

Country Codes:

UK and Northern Ireland: 44

Eire: 353

US: 1

Australia: 61

New Zealand: 64

Within France: outside Paris there are no area codes when making a telephone call; simply dial the 8-digit number.

To call the operator, dial 13; for Directory Enquiries dial 12.

Coins accepted in pay phones are 50 centimes and 1, 5 or 10 francs, though most booths now only take phone cards; you can buy the *télécarte* needed for these booths from post offices and tobacconists.

Time

Local time in France is one hour later than in Britain, except for a short period in autumn and spring when the change to winter or summer time is made. France changes earlier. Eastern US is six hours earlier than France in winter, five in summer; Central Canada is 7 hours earlier than France, 6 in summer.

Tipping

Waiters in bars and cafés are normally left a small tip. In almost all restaurants 15 per cent is added to the bill for gratuities. This is usually indicated by *Prix Nets* or *Service Compris* somewhere on the bill. If it says *Service non compris*, add 15 per cent. You may leave more for exceptional service.

Toilets

Public toilets in France are still few and far between, though they do exist, even in villages sometimes. Many hotels (and better campsites) now have modern toilets, but the more primitive type can still be found in some bars and restaurants, and, surprisingly, at autoroute stops which are not fuel stations. You can always use a toilet in a café or restaurant, but it is reasonable to buy a coffee or a beer. If you see a saucer of small change, a tip is expected.

Tourist Offices

Tourist Information Offices, now usually called *Offices de Tourisme*, though still sometimes *Syndicats d'Initiative*, can be very helpful. They usually have someone who speaks some English, so make full use of them to get details of all local events, amenities and excursions, and even specific information, etc, not available from the larger offices.

National Tourist Offices:

Britain:
French Government Tourist Office, 178 Piccadilly, London WIV 0AL (tel: 0171-491 7622).
United States:
610 Fifth Avenue, Suite 222, New York NY 10020– 2452 (tel: 212/757 1683).
Also offices in Los Angeles, San Francisco, Chicago and Dallas.
Canada:
1981, Avenue Mac-Gill-College, Esso Tower, Suite 490, Montréal, Québec H3A 2W9 (tel: 514/288-4264).
1 Dundas Street West, Suite 2405-Box 8, Toronto, Ontario M5G 1Z3 (tel: 416/593 4717).
Australia:
Kindersley House, 33 Bligh Street, Sydney, NSW 2000 (tel: 2-231 5244).

Tourist Offices in France:

Syndicat d'Initiative, 1 Avenue Aquitaine, Périgueux (tel: 53 53 10 63).
Office de Tourisme, 97 Rue Neuve d'Argenson, Bergerac (tel: 53 57 03 11).
Office de Tourisme, Place Liberté, Sarlat (tel: 53 59 27 67).
In small villages the Mairie (Town Hall) will be able to answer most questions.

LANGUAGE

French people are sticklers for courtesy, and always appreciate it if you try to speak to them in their own language. Here are a few words and phrases which may help those visitors who are not fluent French speakers. Even those who are may have difficulty in understanding a rapid reply in a Périgord accent you could cut with a blunt knife.

please s'il vous plaît (should always be used to get the attention of a stranger, policeman, etc, before asking a question).
hello bonjour
goodbye au revoir
can you direct me to ...? pouvez-vous m'indiquer la direction de ...?
where is ...? où se trouve ...?
how much ...? combien ...?
do you speak English? parlez-vous anglais?
is there anyone here who speaks English? est-ce qu'il y a quelqu'un ici qui parle anglais?
I want to buy je voudrais acheter
that's too expensive c'est trop cher
a room with a bath une chambre avec salle de bains
I did not understand je n'ai pas compris
I have an upset stomach j'ai mal à l'estomac
I have a headache j'ai mal à la tête
is there a good restaurant near here? est-ce qu'il y a un bon restaurant près d'ici?
it's enough c'est assez
the bill, please l'addition, s'il vous plaît

Numbers
one un/une
two deux
three trois
four quatre
five cinq
six six
seven sept
eight huit
nine neuf
ten dix

Days of the Week
Monday lundi
Tuesday mardi
Wednesday mercredi
Thursday jeudi
Friday vendredi
Saturday samedi
Sunday dimanche

Shopping
shops les magasins
baker la boulangerie
newsagents, paper shop, stationers la librairie
library la bibliothèque
butcher la boucherie
chemist la pharmacie
delicatessen la charcuterie
food shop l'alimentation
ironmongers la quincaillerie
fishmongers la poissonnerie
hairdressers salon de coiffure

Health
aspirin de l'aspirine
stomach pills des comprimés digestifs
prescription l'ordonnance
sleeping pills des somnifères

Garage
brakes les freins
engine le moteur
starter le démarreur
ignition l'allumage
clutch l'embrayage
flat tyre un pneu crevé

INDEX

INDEX/ACKNOWLEDGEMENTS

Acknowledgements

The Automobile Association would like to thank the following photographers and libraries for their assistance in the preparation of this book:

BARRIE SMITH took all the photographs in this book (© AA Photo Library) except:
J ALLAN CASH PHOTLIBRARY 12/13 Prehistoric skeleton, 106/7 Sarlat market.
DORDOGNE TOURIST OFFICE 14/15 Lascaux caves.
MARY EVANS PICTURE LIBRARY 18 Eleanor of Aquitaine.
NATURE PHOTGRAPHERS LTD 87 Truffles (E Green), 88 Red-backed shrike (F V Blackburn), 91 Edible Dormouse (O Newman), 92 Map butterfly (F V Blackburn), 93 Short-toed eagle, 95 Purple heron (K J Carlson).
RONALD SHERIDAN'S PHOTO LIBRARY 71 Grotte de Font de Gaume.
SPECTRUM COLOUR LIBRARY Cover Beynac, 75 Monpazier, 121 Folk costume.

Contributors for this revision:
Verifier: Richard Sale; Copy editor: Colin Follett